Information Retrieval System
Service Oriented Architecture (SoA)

Dr. K. Thippeswamy

ELIVA PRESS

Dr. K. Thippeswamy

Retrieval and analysis of information from knowledge base is a basic and vital function that any system is expected to provide with the growing complexity of information. Various institutions/organizations generate valuable information in different domains which is queried and analyzed by users for their purposes. Transporting Reservation, Finance, E-Real estate, Life science, Pharmacy etc, are few of the knowledge driven sectors where data analysis is imperative. Most of the applications performing these tasks are predominantly database driven and tightly coupled with the database system. These limits are the possibilities of seamless database integration with other sources of knowledge and also their ability to create and make changes in the information structures.

Published by Eliva Press SRL
Address: MD-2060, bd.Cuza-Voda, 1/4, of. 21 Chişinău, Republica
Moldova
Email: info@elivapress.com
Website: www.elivapress.com

ISBN: 978-1-63648-068-8

ABSTRACT

Retrieval and analysis of information from knowledgebase is a basic and vital function that any system is expected to provide with the growing complexity of information. Various institutions/organizations generate valuable information in different domains which is queried and analyzed by users for their purposes. Transporting Reservation, Finance, E-Real estate, Life science, Pharmacy etc, are few of the knowledge driven sectors where data analysis is imperative. Most of the applications performing these tasks are predominantly database driven and tightly coupled with the database system. These limits are the possibilities of seamless database integration with other sources of knowledge and also their ability to create and make changes in the information structures.

Through the literature survey done on **"Information Retrieval System"**, it is found that most of the applications are database driven and tightly coupled system. Access the information is tightly coupled, whole structure of the database is exposed to the application, which raising data security problem from organization generated data and integration methodology gets affected when new databases are added. Therefore, the detailed assessment has been planned and carried out for the practical approach of Design and Development of Service Oriented Architecture (SOA) for Information Retrieval System using web services. The design and development of the technical specification of the following modules have to be worked upon to create a loosely coupled system. They are model for relational database representation in Extensible Markup Language (XML) format, model to represent the set of input parameters, model to create web services with an aim to share compatible data framework, model to create loosely coupled system to maintain Enterprise Service Bus (ESB) and information retrieval system which is configurable, adequate and independent of data resources.

Model for Relational database representation in Extensible Markup Language (XML) format have preferred over the traditional delimiter separated file because of the ability of XML to show the hierarchical relations in an effective manner and also due to the flexibility to make changes without affecting the existing structure. An XML schema has been design to represent the tables in a database and the relationships between their tables. The main issues of heterogeneity in terms of column naming have been specified.

Model to represent the set of input parameters, input search query can either in a delimiter separated form or can be in XML form. Match type can be strict where search should go to all the tables or can be search continues if next table, if no match found in current table. The grouping status identified by group and to group according to usage of column.

Model to create web services with an aim to share common data framework, in principle with SOA approach have developed, web services modules which can communicate with the clients and exchange information. The complete configuration has been setup using Apache axis2 engine for developing the web services. Two type of service model were developed which can be used by the clients programs. They are Axis2 Object Model (AXIOM) and Axis2 Data Binding (ADB).

Since XML is the universally accepted method of information exchange, apache axis2 provides a XML object model for efficient Simple Object Access Protocol (SOAP) messaging. Instead of the XML Axiom data object becomes the method of data transfer. This supports novel "pull-through" model to provide turn off the tree building and directly access the underlying pull event stream. It also built in support for XML Optimized Packaging (XOP) and Message Transmission Optimization Mechanism (MTOM), the combination of this allows XML to carry binary data efficiently and invisible manner. The nature of message transfer will be both in and out have to describe appropriate message receiver in the Service.xml file. After receiving the input AXIOM the web services will process the AXIOM and return the appropriate XML file as an AXIOM model.

ADB model is the most advanced model which provides the application to send and receive java objects instead of the AXIOM which they can directly use in the application. The ADB framework provides a linking code from the Web Services Descriptive Language (WSDL) file which can be directly used by the applications. From the WSDL file skeleton code can be generated where later can put the business logic from the existing java code. Connecting code is created by default wsdl4java library. Based on the WSDL the wsdl4java Application Program Interface (API) creates the connecting code known as stub code.

Model to have a loosely coupled system to maintain services, ESB system provides the infrastructure for implementing SOA architecture's acts as intermediary layer between the web services and the client application. Apache synapse is used as the ESB layer because of flexibility in maintaining the configuration files which are in XML format. Any changes in the service configuration file can be done without actually restarting the servers. Since the models of web services need to have Context based routing mechanism by means of synapse routes the incoming message to the appropriate web services.

Generic information retrieval system model to represent the underlying relational database in a standard form, model to generate queries based on input conditions, querying, filtering and grouping across databases. Based on the input query after processing with appropriate parameters output will be dispatched.

Model to perform querying and filtering is designed from the perspective of narrowing down on the most specific record based on the series input data. After input condition is processed, for each search condition corresponding table details are retrieved and stored. Then for each table details queries are formed and data is extracted. Each table query also has the output of previous query as a part of the constraint, thus relating to the previous table.

Model to perform filtering and grouping is done with a prospective of classifying the output by a column which is referred as group by column. This is important from statistical analysis, bar graph etc. Also it is very significant in domains like transporting reservation, E-Real estate, life science, finance etc., and the designed model to perform a grouping operation between two column values not only in the same table but any tables in the system. After the filtering as described in the above step the series of key value pair acting as an output. The details of group by and group to column are searched. Then for each value of group by column subset of the output key value pair is taken and then the corresponding group column is queried in the respective table of group column. So each group can obtain the data of group column which can be taken for next level of grouping.

In this thesis innovated and presented an approach of service oriented architecture for information retrieval system using web services which can be used for querying and analysis with each module being loosely coupled with other. The summary of results achieved in this context independent each other, configurable module and service oriented model.

By reviewing the results and analysis of all the above mentioned existing models, it is found that SOA approaches outperforms all the existing models and proposed models. Hence, it is conclude that the SOA can be used in the design and development of distributed information retrieval system.

Contents

CHAPTER - 1

INTRODUCTION

1.1 Background

Data mining and analysis is a major task in various sectors like business, finance, pharmacy, life sciences, government organization and transport reservation etc., Once information is generated, the foremost task is to integrate and exchange with other organization that use this information with their application for data analysis. Traditional approach consists of physically moving the information to other location or to have a tightly coupled system to use it. It becomes very difficult to maintain such system because of the ever changing information resources. The era of Web2.0 there is increasing need of information exchange across platform, across location on real time basis [1].

Tremendous amount of information is exists at our fingertips. Intelligent and effective use of information becomes a most important key to success. Therefore, wide range of solutions has come out to enhance information retrieval system. According to the tightly coupled information retrieval system integrates the local Database Management Systems (DBMS), these solutions can be further classified. A tightly coupled system means the global functions have access to low-level internal functions of the local DBMS. Main advantages are close synchronization among web sites and efficient global processing. However, it sacrifices web site autonomy, i.e. local DBMSs do not have full control over local resources and this is not desirable. On the other hand, in a more loosely coupled system, the global functions access local functions through the DBMS's external user interface, which enhancing web site autonomy. The existing technologies are begins from the most tightly coupled to the major loosely coupled system [2].

1.2 Existing Technologies

Description of the existing technologies in the field of information retrieval system will be overviewed. This provides the necessary background for justifying the values and the merits of proposed design over the existing ones.

1.2.1 Distributed Databases

A distributed database is the most tightly coupled, i.e. global and local functions share low-level internal interfaces with little distinction. The system typically maintains a global schema created by integrating the schemas of all local DBMSs. A schema is a structured description of the information in a database. Global users then access the system by submitting queries over the global schema [3].

Figure 1.1 shows a general overview of the distributed databases frame work Java Database Connectivity Web Services (JDBC-WS) provides over single kinds of data sources.

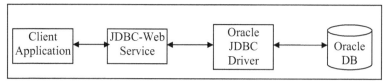

Figure 1.1: Web Services-based access to relational databases

Due to the effect of low level interfaces leads efficiency and performance factor significantly reduce this is overcome in the proposed system.

1.2.2 Global Schema Multidatabases

Since more number of loosely coupled systems global functions access local information through the external user interface of the local DBMS [4]. However, the local sites still need to cooperate closely to maintain a global schema.

The standard levels of global schema approaches have been incorporated with multi databases according to their application domain.

1.2.3 Federated Databases

There is no single global schema, since each local system maintains a local import and export schema. The export schema describes the information shared by the local node. The import schema describes the information (both data representation and data origin) accessible from remote nodes. Therefore, each node only needs to cooperate with specific nodes it accesses.

The tree structural specifications of Federated Database Management Systems (FDBMS) as shown in Figure 1.2, which comprises three important components like centralized DBMS, distributed DBMS and other FDBMS [5].

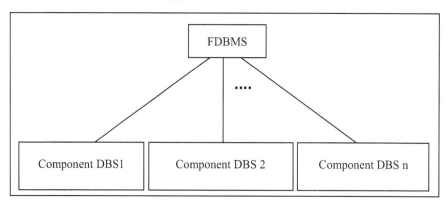

Figure 1.2: Federated Databases System

Multilevel schema provides efficient information scalability which provides universal data accessibility to all set of nodes in federated database.

1.2.4 Multidatabase Language Systems

To enhancement of multi database essentially requires interfacing of language class domain in loosely coupled system. These maintain and support all global database functions with their query language tools to integrate information from separate databases.

The architecture, Global Schema Structured Query Language (SQL) queries are submitted to the Schema SQL server, which determines a series of local SQL queries and submits them to the local databases. The Schema SQL server then collects the answers from local databases and using its own resident SQL engine, executes final series of SQL queries to produce the answer to the global query. Intuitively, the task of the Schema SQL server is to compile the instantiations for the variables declared in the query and enforce the conditions, groupings, aggregations and merging to produce the output. Many query optimization opportunities at different stages and different levels of abstraction are possible and should be employed for efficiency [6]. Figure 1.3 describes the implementation architecture.

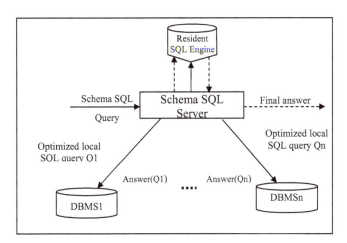

Figure 1.3: Schema SQL - Server

Mainly language systems having formatted application programming interface to integrate the information successfully in a global schema.

1.2.5 Interoperable Systems

The most loosely coupled information sharing systems do not support full database functionality. Since the global system is not database oriented, local systems may include other types of information repositories, such as digital libraries and expert systems.

The current implementation makes it possible to access any of these databases through Common Object Request Broker (CORBA) using global query language based on SQL. When a client application issues a global SQL query to access multiple databases this global query is decomposed into global sub queries and these sub queries are sent to the ORB (CORBAs Object Request Broker) which transfers them to the relevant database servers on the network. On a server side the global sub query is executed by using the corresponding call level interface routines and the result is returned back to the client again by the ORB [7]. The results returned to the client from the related servers are processed by the client if necessary. A general overview of the system is presented in Figure 1.4.

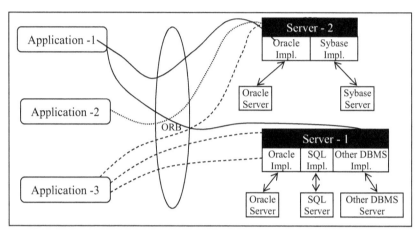

Figure 1.4: Interoperable Overview of the System

The full fledge database functionality can be incorporate with an interfacing functions of interoperability.

1.3   Existing System Problems

The related research work extracting the features of the existing system drawbacks in the domain of information retrieval system. It leads the necessary background for justifying the values and the advantages of the proposed design & development over the existing systems [1-7].

- The structure of the information should be understood and integrate by the application.
- The accessible information applications are tightly coupled.
- Any changes to the database will effects the application program.
- The whole structure of the database is exposed to the application, which raises data security problem from organization generated data.
- Client should have expertise to use and integrate the data.
- An integration methodology gets affected when new databases are added.
- No scope of application to application communication over internet for sharing data structure.

- If another organization want to access the database for different reason then another application must be created to access the database, but the logic may be the same as earlier application program.

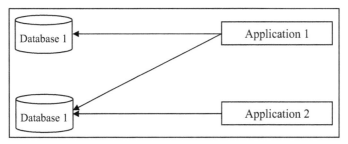

Figure 1.5: Existing System

The above drawbacks of the existing systems have been pictorially represented in Figure 1.5

1.4   Proposed Systems

The proposed SOA for information retrieval system, comprising a loosely coupled system with an ability to perform complex querying, analysis and seamless integration with other systems, both off line and online, they are.

- Creation of a loosely coupled information retrieval system.
- Approach to decompose the application in to services which can operate independently and also communicate each other.
- Client program to access the generic framework services to perform data analysis without dependent on the internal system.
- Interfacing application to application data communication by different abstractions.
- The development of a client module to interact with the services.

    The features of design specifications of proposed system described as mentioned in the Figure 1.6.

The components and requirements assumed for this research work are listed below. The proposed models have few common components at the architectural level. The performance analyses of all models are to be evaluated under the same system environment and IR model.

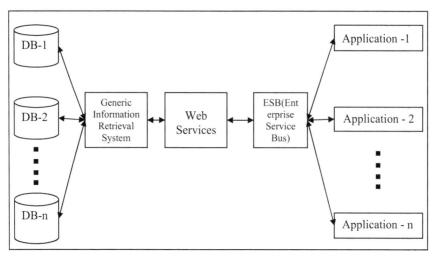

Figure 1.6: Proposed System using SOA

Components: The common components used in the Information Retrieval system architecture models are Service Oriented Architecture (SOA), Web Services, Web Services Description Language (WSDL), Extensible Markup Language (XML), Enterprise Service Bus (ESB) and Database Management Systems (DBMS).

Requirements: The Proposed models are implemented using the following hardware, software and IR models.

(i) **Hardware:** Pentium Dual Core Processor based PC @ 2.4 GHz with 3 GB RAM and 320 GB HDD.

(ii) **Software:** Java2 with Eclipse for Spring IDE and MATLAB6.0

Based on the above methodology and requirements, four models are proposed in this thesis.

1.5   Motivation

Information is a key resource in the daily operation of life science, business, finance, government and academic originations. The organizational information is frequently deposited in digital databases. As organization and users become more sophisticated, interchanging of information resources are also increases. However, the current system limits the access methods and user paradigms [1-7]. Users to learn all these database issues, yet it is also difficult to expect organizations to convert all their systems to a single common data model with a single retrieval method.

The proposed information retrieval system effectively retrieves which provide users a common interface to multiple databases, while minimizing the impact on existing IR system operations. IR systems often provide critical functions and represent significant principal investment. Many institutions/organizations have several types of digital and database systems. In different cases, the environment must be preserved and also addressing the need to share information more universal basis. Integrated retrieval is required to semantically similar information at many nodes and with different data representations. The key motivation factors of proposed research are as follows.

- Multidatabases typically integrate information from preexisting, heterogeneous local databases in a distributed environment and present global users with transparent methods to use the total information in the system.
- A distributed database is the most tightly coupled global information interchanging system.
- Global schema Multidatabases are typically designed bottom-up and can integrate preexisting local DBMS without modifying them.
- Federated databases are more loosely coupled subset of global schema Multidatabases. There is no single global schema each local system maintains its own local import and export schema.
- Interoperable systems are the most loosely coupled information interchanging systems. Global functions are limited to simple data exchange, does not support full database functionality.
- Distributed systems contain a variety of machine types, sizes and small machines should be able to join the systems with minimal local overhead required.
- The investigation on service oriented architecture for information retrieval system has not been done so far.

1.6   Objectives

The main objective of this research work is to develop an Information Retrieval System model that supports the following.

- Information Integration & interchanging among the multiple applications.
- Intercommunication between heterogeneous Databases.
- Information content of information resources collected.
- Utility of information resources.
- Documentary resources.
- Performance resources.
- Users web services.

1.7   Problem Statement

The formal problem descriptions of this research work are to perform a detailed exploration of the Design and Development of Service Oriented Architecture for Information Retrieval using web Services. The description of practical approaches of this research problems have been specified in the following four models.

1. The structure of the information should be understood and integrate by the application and the accessible information applications are tightly coupled. The proposed loosely coupled model to characterize the underlying relational database in a generic form.

2. Any changes to the database will affect the application program and the whole structure of the database is exposed to the application, which raises data security problem from organization generated data. To secure the database and application, proposed a model to symbolize the input query.

3. Client should have expertise to use and integrate the data, and integration methodology gets affected when new databases are added. The proposed model generates queries and dispatch the output based on input constraints, querying, filtering and grouping across databases.

4. Due to the limited scope of applications communication over internet for sharing data structure. If another organization want to access the database for different reason then another application must be created to access the database, but the logic may be the same as earlier application program. The proposed model to provide an effective service interface to communicate with various client applications.

CHAPTER - 2
LITERATURE SURVEY

2.1 Literature Survey on Existing Technology

The amount of data on the internet has been growing at a rate of 10 times for every $3 \sim 4$ years, and many applications handling new data types have been emerging. They include information retrieval (IR), spatial databases, data mining, and data streaming. Accordingly, DBMSs have been evolving to support these new applications. DBMS vendors provide extension mechanisms for adding new data types and operations to their own DBMSs. Examples are Cartridge for Oracle and Extender for IBM DB2. In these products, new data types are added by using user-defined types, their operations by using user defined functions, and their indexes by using extensible indexing. Here, user defined data types, functions, and extensible indexing are implemented through the high-level (typically, SQL-level) interface provided by the DBMS. We call this mechanism as tight-coupling. In the tight -coupling architecture, the high-level interface causes the following problems. First, inter-process communication or dynamic linking overhead is incurred because operations on new data types are performed outside the core DBMS engine. Second, concurrency control and recovery in fine granularity are hard to perform because low-level functions of the DBMS engine cannot be fully utilized for new data types through the high-level interface [1-2].

We have proposed the loosely-coupled service oriented architecture to solve these problems. In the loosely - coupled service oriented architecture, new data types, models and operations are implemented directly into the core of the DBMS engine (i.e., the storage system). Hence, the problems above do not occur in the loosely – coupled service oriented architecture. This loosely - coupled service oriented architecture is being used to incorporate IR and spatial database features into the DBMS. The comparison of various approaches in the existing technology is listed below.

2.1.1 Web Services in Distributed Databases

The current web services framework only provides an infrastructure for building distributed applications utilizing web services infrastructure. Many real-world business requirements such as integrity, automation, transactional support, and security issues are not completely dealt with yet in the current framework [3].

Figure 2.1 shows an overview of the distributed databases framework Java Database Connectivity web services (JDBC-WS) provides multiple data sources.

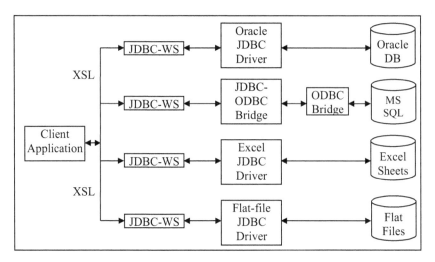

Figure 2.1: Distributed data sources and databases via JDBC-WS

Most of data in the web is currently held in relational database systems today. Web applications simply provide an interface to query and present that data in HTML format to the end user web browsers interpret and display the HTML tagged data in an intended format. Therefore, the data presented in HTML format is not usable by other applications it is more intended for directing the browser to present data for human reading. On the other hand, providing direct access to databases is not feasible due to security, performance, scalability, and reliability issues. There is a need for a standard mechanism to allow applications to access databases just like users access data on databases via web browsers.

This web services approach can in effect be made transparent to the end user who can develop their applications using JDBC. They only need to make a few minor changes like the packages they include and the connection string. This can be achieved by providing client classes that override the existing JDBC classes. For example executing a query in the JDBC application would actually create an XML SOAP request message with the SQL query embedded in the message and that would be sent via HTTP to the remote server where it will be executed. The main advantage of this is that application programmers can use legacy JDBC-based applications with the new JDBC-WS implementation without making many changes.

The effect of low level interfaces leads efficiency and performance factor significantly reduce this is overcome in the proposed system.

2.1.2 Global Schema Multidatabase Systems

Database systems often serve critical functions and represent significant capital investment. Many organizations have several different computers and database systems. In many cases, this environment must be preserved while also addressing the need to share information on a more global basis. Integrated access is required to semantically similar information at different nodes and with different data representations. Multidatabases typically integrate information from preexisting, heterogeneous local databases in a distributed environment and present global users with transparent methods to use the total information in the system. A key feature is the autonomy that individual databases retain to serve their existing customer set.

Multidatabases are an important area of current research, as evidenced by the number of projects in both academia and industry. The trade press has also documented the need for user-friendly global information sharing. The next level of computerization will be distributed global systems that can share information from all participating sites. Multidatabases are a key component of this advancing technology.

Global schema multidatabases are more loosely coupled than distributed databases because global functions access local information through the external user interface of the local DBMS. However, the global system still maintains a global schema, so the local sites must cooperate closely to maintain the global schema. Global schema multi databases are typically designed bottom-up and can integrate preexisting local DBMSs without modifying them. They also normally integrate heterogeneous local DBMSs. This heterogeneity may mean different data models or different implementations of the same data model. Thus, creating the global schema is a more difficult problem than in a distributed database, where the local DBMSs are homogeneous and the global database administrator (DBA) has control over the local schema input to the global schema.

A key aspect of multidatabases, as opposed to distributed databases, is that each local DBMS retains complete control over local data and processing. This is called site autonomy.' Each site independently determines what information it will share with the global system, what global requests it will service, when it will join the multidatabase, and when it will stop participating in it. The DBMS itself is not modified by joining the multidatabase. Neither global changes, such as addition and deletion of other sites, nor global optimization of data structures and processing methods has any effect on the local DBMS. Local DBAs are free to optimize local data structures, access paths, and query-processing methods to satisfy local user requirements rather than global requirements. Since the global system interfaces with the local DBMS at the user level. The local DBMS sees the global system as just another local user. Note that site autonomy applies to the local DBMS rather than the local system as a whole. The local system must support some subset of the global function.

The multidatabase approach of preserving site autonomy may be desirable for several reasons. Some local databases may have critical roles in an organization, and it may be impossible from an economic standpoint to change these systems. Site autonomy means the local DBMS can add global access without changing this existing local function. Another economic factor is that an organization may have significant capital invested in existing hardware, software and user training. All of this investment is preserved when joining a multi database because existing local applications can continue operating unchanged. Site autonomy can also act as a security measure because the local DBMS has full control over who accesses local resources through the multidatabase interface and what processing options will be allowed. In particular, a site can protect information by not including it in the local schema that is shared with the global system. An organization's requirement for global access may be minimal or sporadic. Site autonomy allows the local DBMS to join and quit the multidatabase with minimal local impact [4].

Tables 2.1 review most of the current multidatabase projects reported in the literature. These projects come from a variety of countries and institutions. Some are mainly research vehicles to study specific problem areas; others are full commercial systems. The range of organizations and the number of projects indicate the importance of this field. The tables compare high-level details and include a primary reference for each project.

System Name/Organization	Stage of Development	Global Data Model	Global Updates?	System Emphases or Key Features
ADDS(Amoeo Distributed Database System)'	Limited	Extended	Yes	Comprehensive function, powerful
Amoco Research Center	prototype	relational	Yes	user interface. global constraints
Dataplex-	Limited	Relational	Yes	Query decomposition and
General Motors Research	prototype	Relational	Yes	optimization
DQS (Distributed Query System)'	Prototype	Relational	No	Query optimization
COOS (Experimental Distributed Database System)	Prototype	Relational	Yes	Small machines ean join system
HD-DBMS (Heterogeneous Distributed-DBMS)' UCLA	Research	Entity-relationship	Yes	Global access path information, external views in multiple data models
JDDBS (Japanese Distributed Database System)" Japan Information Processing	Limited prototype	Relational	Yes	Based on a broadcast network
Development Center Mermaid' Unisys Multibase"	Prototype	Relational	No	Query optimization
Computer Corporation of America MulriStar"	Prototype	Relational	No	Query processing, ability to link to other multidatabases
Consortium headed by CRAI, Italy NOMS (Network Data Management System)"	Prototype	Relational	Yes	Oueryoptimization

CRAI, Italy Preci'"				
University of Aherdeen	prototype	conceptual	Yes	different levels of globa I function global access languages
Universities of Paris and Turin INRIA, France	prototype	relationship	Yes	between system levels
XNDM (Experimental Network Data Manager)	Limited prototype	Relational	Yes	Data translations, use of server nodes for global processing

Table 2.1: Global Schema Multidatabase Projects [4].

2.1.3   Federated Database Systems

A federated database system (FDBS) is a collection of cooperating but autonomous component database systems (DBSs). The component DBSs are integrated to various degrees. The software that provides controlled and coordinated manipulation of the component DBSs is called a federated database management system (FDBMS). Both databases and DBMSs play important roles in defining the architecture of an FDBS. Component database refers to a database of a component DBS. A component DBS can participate in more than one federation. The DBMS of a component DBS, or component DBMS, can be a centralized or distributed DBMS or another FDBMS. The component DBMSs can differ in such aspects as data models, query languages, and transaction management capabilities. One of the significant aspects of an FDBS is that a component DBS can continue its local operations and at the same time participate in a federation. The integration of component DBSs may be managed either by the users of the federation or by the administrator of the FDBS together with the administrators of the component DBSs. The amount of integration depends on the needs of federation users and desires of the administrators of the component DBSs to participate in the federation and share their databases.

The tree structural specifications of Federated Database Management Systems (FDBMS) and its components are shown in Figure 2.2, which comprises three important components like centralized DBMS, distributed DBMS and other type of FDBMS [5].

Identifying and representing all semantics useful in performing various FDBS tasks such as schema translation and schema integration and determining contents of schemas at various levels. Lack of software tools to aid in performing various FDBS tasks with a high degree of automation and an integrated toolset for developing, maintaining, and managing FDBSs.

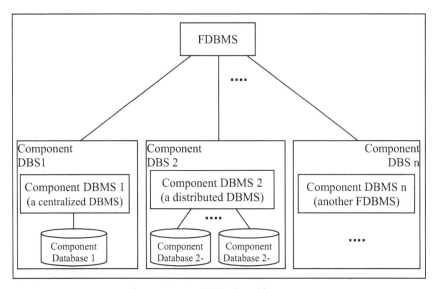

Figure 2.2: An FDBMS and its components

2.1.4 Multidatabase Language Systems

One of the fundamental requirements in a multidatabase Language system is interoperability, which is the ability to uniformly share, interpret, and manipulate information in component databases in a MDBS. Almost all factors of heterogeneity in a MDBS pose challenges for interoperability [6]. These factors can be classified into semantics issues (e.g., interpreting and cross-relating information in different local databases), syntactic issues (e.g., heterogeneity in database schemas, data models, and in query processing, etc.), and systems issues (e.g., operating systems, communication protocols, consistency management, security management, etc). We focus on syntactic issues here. We consider the problem of interoperability among a number of component relational databases storing semantically similar information in structurally dissimilar ways.

Figure 2.3 depicts our architecture for implementing SchemaSQL. Query processing in a SchemaSQL environment consists of two major phases. In the first phase, tables called Variable Instantiation Table (VIT) corresponding to the variable declaration in the from clause of a SchemaSQL statement are generated. The schema of a VIT consist of all the variables in one or more variable declarations in the from clause and its contents correspond to instantiations of these variables. VIT's are materialized by executing appropriate SQL queries on the FST and/or component databases. In the second phase, the SchemaSQL query is rewritten into an equivalent SQL query on the VIT's and the generated answer is ppropriately presented to the user. Our algorithm below considers SchemaSQL queries with a fixed output schema possibly with aggregation.

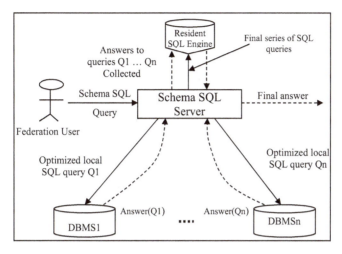

Figure 2.3: Schema SQL - Implementation Architecture

We compare and contrast our proposal against some of the related work for meta-data manipulation and multidatabase interoperability. The features of SchemaSQL that distinguishes it from similar works include.

- Uniform treatment of data and metadata.
- No explicit use of object identifiers.
- Downward compatibility with SQL.
- Comprehensive aggregation facility.
- Restructuring views, in which data and meta-data may be interchanged.
- Designed specifically for interoperability in multidatabase systems.

2.1.5 Interoperable Database Systems

Commercially available technology offers inadequate support both for integrated access to multiple databases and for integrating multiple applications into a comprehensive framework. Some products offer dedicated gateways to other DBMSs with limited capabilities. Thus, they require a complete change of the organizational structure of existing databases to cope with heterogeneity.

Another way of achieving interoperability among heterogeneous databases is through a multidatabase system. A multidatabase system (MDBS) [7] is a database system that drives other database systems and allows the users to simultaneously access independent databases using a single data definition and manipulation language. The primary objective of a MDBS is to significantly enhance productivity in developing and executing applications that require simultaneous access against multiple independent databases. A multidatabase system provides a single global schema that represents an integration of the relevant portions of the underlying local databases. The users may formulate queries and updates against the global schema.

2.2 Literature Survey on Service Oriented Architecture

The widespread emergence of the Internet in the mid 1990s as a platform for electronic data distribution and the advent of structured information have revolutionized our ability to deliver information to any corner of the world. While the introduction of Extensible Markup Language (XML) as a structured format was a major enabling factor, the promise offered by SOAP based web services triggered the discovery of architectural patterns that are now known as Service Oriented Architecture (SOA) [8,9,10].

Service Oriented Architecture is an architectural paradigm and discipline that is used to build infrastructures enabling those with needs of consumers and those with capabilities of providers to interact via services across disparate domains of technology and ownership. Services act as the core facilitator of electronic data interchanges yet require additional mechanisms in order to function. Several new trends in the computer industry rely upon SOA as the enabling foundation. These include the automation of Business Process Management (BPM), composite applications that aggregate multiple services to function and the multitude of new architecture and design patterns generally referred to as Web 2.0 [11].

The latter Web 2.0 is not defined as a static architecture. Web 2.0 can be generally characterized as a common set of architecture and design patterns, which can be implemented in multiple contexts. The list of common patterns includes the Mashup, Collaboration-Participation, Software as a Service (SaaS), Semantic Tagging (folksonomy) and Rich User Experience (also known as Rich Internet Application) patterns among others. These are augmented with themes for software architects such as trusting users and harnessing collective intelligence [12-18]. Most Web 2.0 architecture patterns rely on Service Oriented Architecture in order to function.

When designing Web 2.0 applications based on these patterns, architects often have highly specialized requirements for moving data. Enterprise adoption of these patterns requires special considerations for scalability, flexibility (in terms of multiple message exchange patterns) and the ability to deliver these services to a multitude of disparate consumers. Architects often need to expand data interchanges beyond simple request-response patterns and adopt more robust message exchange patterns triggered by multiple types of events. As a result many specialized platforms are evolving to meet these needs [19-20].

2.2.1 A Reference Architecture for Service Oriented Architecture

Reference architecture is a more concrete artifact used by architects. Unlike the reference model it can introduce additional details and concepts to provide a more complete picture for those who may implement a particular class. Reference architectures declare details that would be in all instances of a certain class much like an abstract constructor class in programming. The subsequent architecture designed from the reference architecture would be specialized for a specific set of requirements. Reference architectures often introduce concepts such as cardinality, structure, infrastructure and other types of binary relationships. Accordingly, reference models do not have service providers and consumers. If they did then a reference model would have infrastructure between the two concrete entities and it would no longer be a model [21].

The concepts and relationships defined by the reference model are intended to be the basis for describing reference architectures that will define more specific categories of SOA designs. Specifically, these specialized architectures will enable solution patterns to solve particular problems. Concrete architectures may be developed based upon a combination of reference architectures, architectural patterns and additional requirements including those imposed by technology environments [22-25]. Architecture is not done in isolation it must account for the goals, motivation and requirements that define the actual problems being addressed. While reference architectures can form the basis of classes of solutions, concrete architectures will define specific solution approaches.

Architects and developers also need to bind their own SOA to concrete standards technologies and protocols at some point. These are typically part of the requirements process. For example, when building a highly efficient client side Mashup application, a developer might opt for the Action Script Messaging Format (ASMF) to provide the most efficient communication between remote services and the client.

The reference architecture shown in Figure 2.4 is not tied to any specific technologies, standards or protocols. In fact it would be equally applicable to a .NET or J2EE environment and can be used with either the Web Service family of technologies, plain old XML-RPC (XML – Remote Procedure Call) or a proprietary set of standards. This reference architecture allows developers to make decisions and adopt technologies that are best suited to their specific requirements [26].

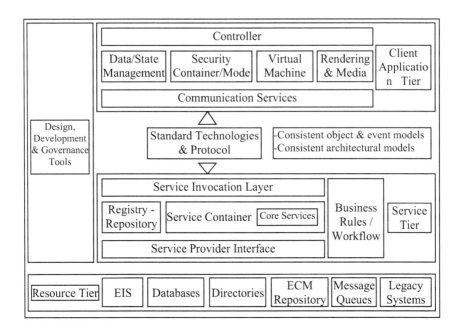

Figure 2.4: A generic SOA Reference Architecture for implementing core Web 2.0 Design patterns

Service Tier

The server side component of the reference architecture has a number of commonly used components. The service provider interface is the main integration point where by service providers connect to capabilities that exist in internal systems in order to expose them as services. These internal applications typically reside in a resource tier, a virtual collection of capabilities that become exposed as services so consumers can access their functionality. Service providers may integrate such capabilities using numerous mechanisms including using other services. In most cases, an enterprise will use the Application Programmatic Interface (API) of the system as provided by the application vendor.

The service invocation layer is where services are invoked. A service may be invoked when an external messages being received or alternatively it can be invoked by an internal system or by a non-message based event (such as a time out). It is essential to understand that services may be invoked via messages from multiple sets of standards and protocols working together. Common examples of external service interface endpoints includes

- Asynchronous JavaScript and XML (AJAX).

- Simple Object Access Protocol (SOAP).

- XML Remote Procedure Call (XML-RPC).

Services may also be invoked by local consumers including environments like J2EE and language specific interfaces for example Plain Old Java Objects (POJO).

Each service invocation is often handed to a new instance of a service container. The service container is responsible for handling the service invocation request for its entire lifecycle until either it reaches a successful conclusion or failed end state. Regardless of its ultimate end state the service container may also delegate responsibilities for certain aspects of the services runtime to other services for common tasks. These tasks typically include logging functions, archiving, security, and authentication among others.

To facilitate orchestration and aggregation of services into processes and composite applications a registry-repository is often used. During the process design phase the registry-repository provides a single view of all services and related artifacts. The repository provides a persistence mechanism for artifacts during the runtime of processes and workflows. If multiple system actors use and interact with a form, the repository can persist it's while allowing access to privileged individuals.

Design, development and governance tools are also commonly used by humans to deploy, monitor and aggregate multiple services into more complex processes and applications.

Client Tier

While much attention has been focused on the server side aspects of SOA less has been written about the new breed of clients evolving for consuming services. The clients have evolved to embrace many common architecture and design patterns discussed in greater detail in the next section. A highly visible example of this is the ability of most modern browsers to subscribe to RSS feeds.

The main controller of each client application must be capable of launching various runtime environments. This is typically done via launching one or more virtual machines that can interpret scripting languages or consume byte code as in Adobe Flash. The architecture for these virtual machines varies greatly depending upon the language used. Some compile an intermediate level byte code just in time to run a program while others must be launched and make multiple passes over a script usually once to check it for errors, another time to run the script and a concurrent iteration to collect garbage and free up memory as it becomes possible to reallocate.

Most modern clients have some form of data persistence and state management. This usually works in conjunction with the client's communications services to allow the controller to use cached resources rather than attempting to synchronize states if communications are down.

Additionally, rendering and media functionality specific to one or more languages is used to ensure the view of the application is built in accordance with the intentions of the application developer.

The security models used by different clients also vary somewhat. The usual tenets are to prevent unauthorized and undetected manipulation of local resources. In distributed computing architectures, identity (knowing who and what) is a major problem that requires a complex architecture to address. Each client side application must be architected in accordance with the acceptable level of risk based on the user requirements.

2.2.2 Loose Coupling

Coupling refers to the number of dependencies between modules. There are two types of coupling they are loose coupling and tight. Loosely coupled modules have a few well-known dependencies. Tightly coupled modules have many unknown dependencies. All software architecture strives to achieve loose coupling between modules. Service-oriented architecture promotes loose coupling between service consumers and service providers and the idea of a few well-known dependencies between consumers and providers. A system's degree of coupling directly affects its modifiability. The more tightly coupled system is, the more a change in a service will require changes in service consumers. Coupling is increased when service consumers require a large amount of information about the service provider to use the service [27-30]. In other words, if a service consumer knows the location and detailed data format for a service provider, the consumer and provider are more tightly coupled. If the consumer of the service does not need detailed knowledge of the service before invoking it, the consumer and provider are more loosely coupled.

SOA accomplishes loose coupling through the use of contracts and bindings. A consumer asks a third-party registry for information about the type of service it wishes to use. The registry returns all the services it has available that match the consumer's criteria. The consumer chooses which service to use binds to it over a transport and executes the method on it based on the description of the service provided by the registry. The consumer does not depend directly on the service's implementation but only on the contract the service supports. Since a service may be both a consumer and a provider of some services, the dependency on only the contract enforces the notion of loose coupling in service-oriented architecture. Although coupling between service consumers and service producers is loose, implementation of the service can be tightly coupled with implementation of other services. For instance, if a set of services shares a framework, a database, or otherwise has information about each other's implementation, they may be tightly coupled. In many instances coupling cannot be avoided and it sometimes contradicts the goal of code reusability.

2.3   SOA Significant Features

Today's IT organizations invariably employ disparate systems and technologies. Most analysts predict that J2EE and .NET will continue to coexist in most organizations and the trend of having heterogeneous technologies in IT shops. Moreover, creating applications that leverage these different technologies has historically been a daunting task. SOA provides a clear solution to these application integration issues by allowing systems to expose their functionality via standardized, interoperable interfaces [31-35]. Using SOA offers several key advantages.

- Adapt applications to change in technologies.
- Easily integrate applications with other systems.
- Leverage existing investments in legacy applications.
- Quickly and easily create a business process from existing services.

2.3.1   SOA and Java

Most developers often think web services and SOA are synonymous. Most of the organization thinks it's not possible to build service-oriented applications without using web services. To clarify, SOA is a design principle, whereas web services are implementation technology. User *can* build a service-oriented application without using web services for example, by using other traditional technologies such as Java RMI.

The main theme behind SOA is to find the appropriate modularity and achieve loose coupling between modules. User can build an application where the modules don't have vast tight coupling between interacting components, such as an application where the JSP presentation layer is not tightly integrated with the data model and accesses it appropriately via an Enterprise Java Beans (EJB).

It's worth mentioning that Jini had long established the concept of SOA prior to the rise in popularity of web services. Web services bring to the table of the platform-independent standards such as Hypertext Transfer Protocol (HTTP), XML, SOAP and Universal Description Discovery and Integration (UDDI), which allows interoperability between heterogeneous technologies such as J2EE and .NET.

2.3.2   SOA and OSI

Contrast of SOA and OSI architecture discuss similarities and differences between the two, synthesizing the logical components of both architectures in Table 2.2. With this comparison user want to show that SOA principles have been present in telecommunications for a while, and their implementation becomes more advanced as technology improves, evolving from telecommunications services over service-independent platforms to web service technologies.

In SOA, services are software resources, each service having its distinct functional context. A combination of these services can be dynamically composed in a composite service, resulting in added value functionality. In Open Systems Interconnection (OSI), services also have distinct functional roles, each service being a set of primitives that provides communication functionality in order to interconnect open standard systems.

SOA		OSI	
Logical Compone nt	**Description**	**Logical Component**	**Description**
Service	**is** a software resource. **provides** business functionality. **communicates** with other services **has** a *published* interface **is described** in a standard definition language	Service	**is** a set of primitives **provides** communication functionality **communicates** with services on *adjacent* layers **has** an interface —
Interface	**defines** the identity of a service and its invocation logistics	Interface	**specifies** what the parameters are and what results to expect
Message	**is** a formatted service request or service response **can be** anything useful to a business	Primitive	**is** a formatted service request or service response **is** an agreement between the communicating parties on how communication is to proceed **is** a set of rules governing the format and meaning of the packets that are exchanged by the peer entities within a layer
Functional ity	**is used** by entities to implement their service definitions **is** implemented in software	Protocol	**is used** by entities to implement their service definitions **may be** implemented in hardware, software, or a combination of the two

Table 2.2: Comparison of the logical components of SOA and OSI models

These primitives can make use of both software and hardware resources, making the definition of a service in OSI broader. On the other hand, the purpose of a service in SOA is to provide business functionality, so therefore it is broader than in OSI. Furthermore, in SOA services have three essential properties: they are self-contained, platform-independent, and can be dynamically located, invoked, and recombined. In OSI however services are statically defined and invoked and cannot be recombined. Recent research in dynamically composing protocol stacks and layers can be seen as an attempt to apply SOA principles to communication networks, therefore breaking or enhancing OSI principles such as communication restricted to adjacent layers by cross-layer interactions. In SOA, interfaces to services define the identity of the service and its invocation logistics through a standard language that can be understood by a machine (e.g., Web Service Description Language). Then this information is published to facilitate dynamic discovery. None of these apply to OSI interfaces, which are statically defined as a result of long standardization processes. In OSI, layer N can only request a service using service primitives (i.e., means for interlayer communication between service requestor and service provider) from layer $N - 1$. Services in OSI refer to communication services and use protocols to achieve their functionality.

	SOA	OSI
Model	Yes	Yes
Modularity	Yes	Yes
Decoupling	Yes	Yes
Dynamic composition	Yes	No
Implemented as is	No	No
Implementation	Web services	ISDN, GSM

Table 2.3: Key similarities and differences between the SOA and OSI models

Entities on the same layer use these protocols to move the information from one machine to another. However services are decoupled from protocols so they can use any protocol as long as they perform the same functionality and use the same interfaces. In SOA, services of different types can communicate with other services via messages, which can be seen as equivalent to primitives in the OSI model. Making use of this communication the composition of services can be performed based on the needed functionality not in a static predefined manner. The service functionality and the manner in which they discover other useful services are transparent to third parties similar to the way protocols used by the underlying layer are transparent to the client layer in OSI architecture [36-40].

The functionality of a service in SOA is logically equivalent to the protocol for providing communication functionality in OSI. Both SOA and OSI are theoretical models that assume a modular structure and follow a loose coupling principle that calls for clear separation of services from their implementation. While OSI has a clear vertical structure SOA can be both horizontal and vertical. The main difference between the two models (Table 2.3) is that SOA refers to dynamic composition of services while OSI defines only two types of services (connection-oriented and connectionless) and seven functional layers. SOA is also an interconnection architecture as it refers to interconnecting software systems into business applications. It is important to note that neither of the two models has been implemented as defined [41-50]. The dominant implementation of communication architecture is the *Transmission Control Protocol/Internet Protocol* (TCP/IP) stack, while thus far the only implementation of architecture for business functionality seems to be Web services.

2.4 Different Layers for Service-Oriented Applications

Like any distributed application service-oriented applications are multi-tier applications and have presentation, business logic and persistence layers.

Figure 2.5 provides typical service architecture for a service-oriented application. The two key tiers in SOA are the services layer and the business process layer [51-54].

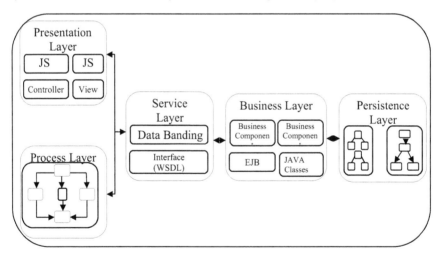

Figure 2.5: Different Layers of Service Oriented Applications

2.4.1 The Service Layer

As we discussed earlier services are the building blocks of service-oriented applications. Thus services are somewhat analogous to Java objects and components such as EJBs. Unlike objects however services are self-contained, maintain their own state, and provide a loosely coupled interface.

The greatest challenge of building a service-oriented application is creating an interface with the right level of abstraction. While analyzing your business requirements carefully considers what software components you want to build as a service. Generally services should provide coarse-grained functionality. For example the software component that processes a purchase order is a good candidate for publication as a service as opposed to a component that just updates an attribute of a purchase order.

You have two choices when building a service: the top-down approach or the bottom-up approach. The top-down approach requires that you identify and describe the messages and operations your service provides and then implement the service. This approach is recommended when you're building a completely new service as it lets you choose your preferred implementation technology. This approach also promotes the most interoperable services since you can avoid implementation artifacts that may preclude interoperability (for example data types that may not have an interoperable representation).

The bottom-up approach is quite popular because it lets you reuse your existing investment in business components. For example, vendors provide the tools that let you expose a PL/SQL-stored procedure that checks whether a customer is entitled to a discount as a service.

The most important aspect of a service is the service description. When using web services as the implementation technology for SOA, Web Services Description Language (WSDL) describes the messages, types and operations of the web service and is the contract to which the web service guarantees it will conform.

2.5   Web Services

First, defining Web Services using Web Services Description Language (WSDL) will be reviewed. That will be followed by SOAP, which provides means of sending messages [55-60].

2.5.1   Using the Web Services Description Language

The Web Services Description Language (WSDL) forms the basis for web services. The following Figure 2.6 illustrates the use of WSDL. At the left is a service provider. At the right is a service consumer. The steps involved in providing and consuming services are.

1. A service provider describes its service using WSDL. This definition is published to a directory of services. The directory could use Universal Description Discovery and Integration (UDDI). Other forms of directories can also be used.
2. A service consumer issues one or more queries to the directory to locate a service and determine how to communicate with that service.
3. Part of the WSDL provided by the service provider is passed to the service consumer. This tells the service consumer what the requests and responses are for the service provider.
4. The service consumer uses the WSDL to send a request to the service provider.

5. The service provider provides the expected response to the service consumer.

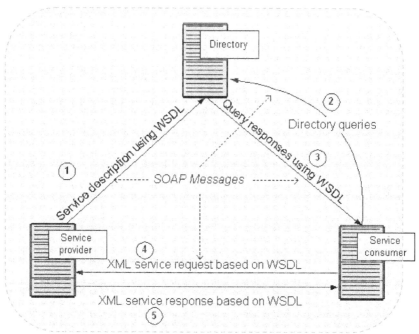

Figure 2.6: Use of Web Services Description Language

2.5.2   Using Universal Description Discovery and Integration (UDDI)

The directory shown in the above Figure 3.4 could be a UDDI registry. The UDDI registry is intended to eventually serve as a means of "discovering" Web Services described using WSDL. The idea is that the UDDI registry can be searched in various ways to obtain contact information and the web services available for various organizations. How much "discovery" will be used in the early days of web services is open to discussion. Nevertheless even without the discovery portion the UDDI registry is a way to keep up-to-date on the web services your organization currently uses. An alternative to UDDI is the XML Registry.

2.5.3   Using SOAP

All the messages shown in the above Figure 3.4 are sent using SOAP. (SOAP at one time stood for Simple Object Access Protocol. Now, the letters in the acronym have no particular meaning) SOAP essentially provides the envelope for sending the web services messages. SOAP generally uses HTTP but other means of connection may be used. HTTP is the familiar connection we all use for the Internet. In fact it is the pervasiveness of HTTP connections that will help drive the adoption of web services.

The Figure 3.5 provides more detail on the messages sent using web services. At the left of the Figure 3.5 is a fragment of the WSDL sent to the directory. It shows a CustomerInfoRequest that requires the customer's account to object information. Also shown is the CustomerInfoResponse that provides a series of items on customer including name, phone and address items.

At the right of this Figure 2.7 is a fragment of the WSDL being sent to the service consumer. This is the same fragment sent to the directory by the service provider. The service consumer uses this WSDL to create the service request shown above the arrow connecting the service consumer to the service provider. Upon receiving the request, the service provider returns a message using the format described in the original WSDL. That message appears at the bottom of the figure.

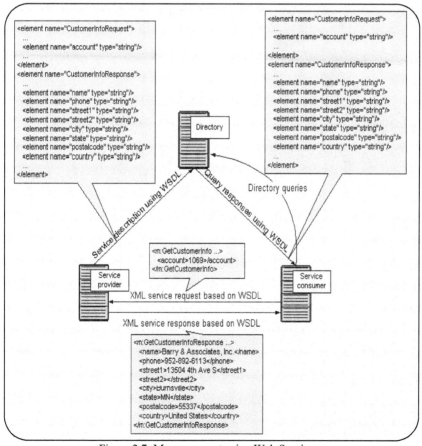

Figure 2.7: Messages sent using Web Services

2.5.4   Using XML with WSDL

WSDL uses XML to define messages. XML has a tagged message format. This is shown in the above Figure 2.7. The tag **<city>** has the value of **Burnsville**. And **</city>** is the ending tag indicating the end of the value of city. Both the service provider and service consumer use these tags. In fact, the service provider could send the data shown at the bottom of this figure in any order. The service consumer uses the tags and not the order of the data to get the data values.

2.5.5   Simplified Web Services Notation

Simplified notation will be used for web services. This is shown below the simplified notation; the directory is implicit in the wide rectangle labeled "Web Services" at the top of this figure. You could think of web services much like the bus in a PC in which you plug various circuit boards. Other middleware solutions appear similar and use the same "bus" concept.

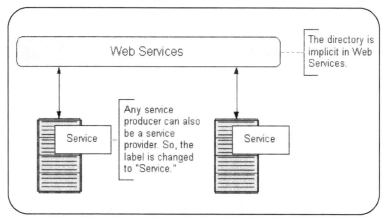

Figure 2.8: Web Services

Another important concept in service-oriented architectures is that any service provider could also be a service consumer. This is why the Figure 2.8 shows only services at the bottom of the figure under the web services bus rather than a "service provider" and a "service consumer".

2.6   Other SOA Concepts

Architectures can operate independently of specific technologies. Designers can implement SOA using a wide range of technologies, including.

- SOAP & RPC
- REST
- DCOM
- CORBA
- Web Services
- DDS
- WCF (Microsoft's implementation of web services now forms a part of WCF)

Implementations can use one or more of these protocols for example, might use a file-system mechanism to communicate data conforming to a defined interface specification between processes conforming to the SOA concept [60-70]. The key is independent services with defined interfaces that can be called to perform their tasks in a standard way without a service having foreknowledge of the calling application and without the application having or needing knowledge of how the service actually performs its tasks.

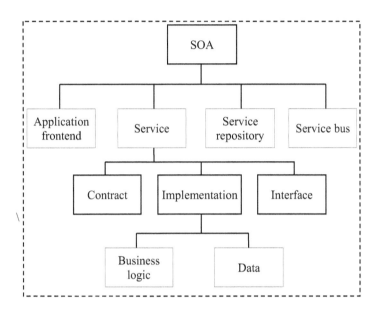

Figure 2.9: Elements of SOA

Many implementers of SOA have begun to adopt an evolution of SOA concepts into a more advanced architecture called SOA 2.0. Figure 2.9 shows elements of SOA.

SOA enables the development of applications that are built by combining loosely coupled and interoperable services. These services inter-operate based on a formal definition (or contract, e.g., WSDL) that is independent of the underlying platform and programming language. The interface definition hides the implementation of the language-specific service. SOA based systems can therefore function independently of development technologies and platforms (such as Java, .NET, etc.). Services written in C# running on .NET platforms and services written in Java running on Java EE platforms, for example can both be consumed by a common composite application (or client) [71-80]. Applications running on either platform can also consume services running on the other as web services that facilitate reuse. Managed environments can also wrap COBOL legacy systems and present them as software services. This has extended the useful life of many core legacy systems indefinitely no matter what language they originally used.

SOA can support integration and consolidation activities within complex enterprise systems but SOA does not specify or provide a methodology or framework for documenting capabilities or services.

High-level languages such as *Business Process Execution Language* (BPEL) and specifications such as Web Services Choreography Description Language (WS-CDL) and WS-Coordination extend the service concept by providing a method of defining and supporting orchestration of fine-grained services into more coarse-grained business services, which architects can in turn incorporate into workflows and business processes implemented in composite applications or portals.

Service-oriented modeling is a SOA framework that identifies the various disciplines that guide SOA practitioners to conceptualize, analyze, design and architect their service-oriented assets. Figure 2.10 shows the Service-Oriented Modeling Framework (SOMF) offers a modeling language and a work structure or "map" depicting the various components that contribute to a successful service-oriented modeling approach. It illustrates the major elements that identify the "what to do" aspects of a service development scheme. The model enables practitioners to craft a project plan and to identify the milestones of a service-oriented initiative. SOMF also provides a common modeling notation to address alignment between business and IT organizations [81-90].

SOMF addresses the following principles:
- Business traceability.
- Architectural best-practices traceability.
- Technological traceability.
- SOA value proposition.
- Software assets reuse.
- SOA integration strategies.
- Technological abstraction and generalization.
- Architectural components abstraction.

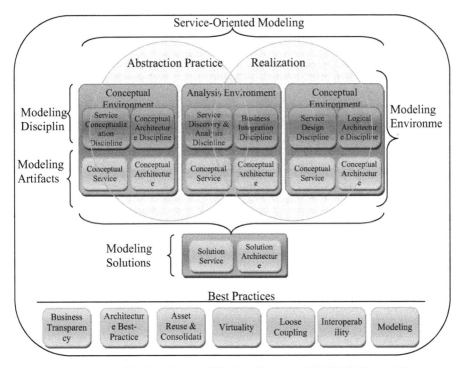

Figure 2.10: Service-Oriented Modeling Framework (SOMF) Version2.0

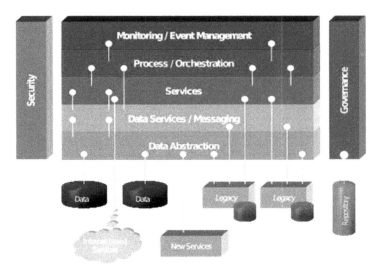

Figure 2.11: SOA meta-model

As in Figure 2.12 example, an enterprise employing SOA could create a supply chain composite application using a set of existing applications that expose the functionality via standard interfaces.

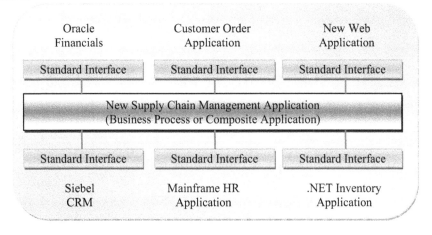

Figure 2.12: Supply chain applications

2.6.1 Service Architecture

To implement SOA, enterprises need a service architecture an example of which is shown in Figure 3.11.

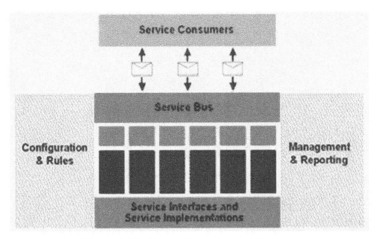

Figure 2.13: A sample service architecture

In Figure 2.13 several service consumers can invoke services by sending messages. These messages are typically transformed and routed by a service bus to an appropriate service implementation. This service architecture can provide a business rules engine that allows business rules to be incorporated in a service or across services. The service architecture also provides a service management infrastructure that manages services and activities like auditing, billing and logging [91-100]. In addition, the architecture offers enterprises the flexibility of having agile business processes better addresses the regulatory requirements like Sarbanes Oxley (SOX) and changes individual services without affecting other services.

2.6.2   SOA Infrastructure

To run and manage SOA applications, enterprises need an SOA infrastructure that is part of the SOA platform. An SOA infrastructure must support all the relevant standards and required runtime containers. A typical SOA infrastructure looks like Figure 2.14. The following sections discuss the infrastructure's individual pieces.

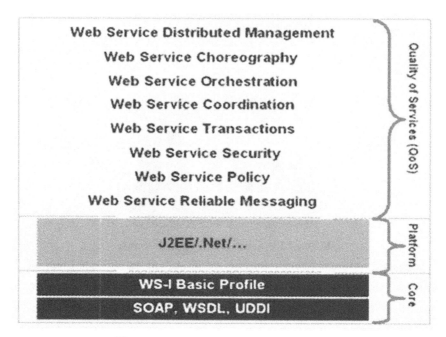

Figure 2.14: A typical SOA infrastructure.

SOAP, WSDL and UDDI

WSDL, UDDI, and SOAP are the fundamental pieces of the SOA infrastructure. WSDL is used to describe the service; UDDI, to register and look up the services; and SOAP as a transport layer to send messages between service consumer and service provider. While SOAP is the default mechanism for web services alternative technologies accomplish other types of bindings for a service. A consumer can search for a service in the UDDI registry, get the WSDL for the service that has the description and invoke the service using SOAP.

WS-I Basic Profile

WS-I Basic Profile, provided by the Web services Interoperability Organization, is turning into another core piece required for service testing and interoperability. Service providers can use the Basic Profile test suites to test a service's interoperability across different platforms and technologies.

J2EE and .Net

Though the J2EE and .Net platforms are the dominant development platforms for SOA applications, SOA is not by any means limited to these platforms. Platforms such as J2EE not only provide the framework for developers to naturally participate in the SOA, but also, by their inherent nature, bring a mature and proven infrastructure for scalability, reliability, availability and performance to the SOA world. Newer specifications such as Java API for XML Binding (JAXB) used for mapping XML documents to Java classes, Java API for XML Registry (JAXR) used for interacting with the UDDI registries in a standard manner and Java API for XML-based Remote Procedure Call (XML-RPC), used for invoking remote services in J2EE 1.4 facilitate the development and deployment of web services that are portable across standard J2EE containers, while simultaneously interoperating with services across other platforms such as .NET.

2.6.3 Quality of Services

Existing mission-critical systems in enterprises address advanced requirements such as security, reliability and transactions. As enterprises start adopting service architecture as a vehicle for developing and deploying applications basic web services specifications like WSDL, SOAP and UDDI aren't going to fulfill these advanced requirements. As mentioned previously these requirements are also known as quality of services. Numerous specifications related to QoS are being worked out in standard bodies like the World Wide Web Consortium (W3C) and the Organization for the Advancement of Structured Information Standards (OASIS). Sections below discuss some of the QoS artifacts and related standards.

Security

The Web Services Security specification addresses message security. This specification focuses on credential exchange, message integrity and message confidentiality. The attractive thing about this specification is it leverages existing security standards, such as Security Assertion Markup Language (SAML), and allows the usage of these standards to secure web services messages. Web Services security is an ongoing OASIS effort.

Reliability

In a typical SOA environment, several documents are exchanged between service consumers and service providers. Delivery of messages with characteristics like once-and-only-once delivery, at-most-once delivery, duplicate message elimination, guaranteed message delivery, and acknowledgment become important in mission-critical systems using service architecture. WS-Reliability and WS-Reliable Messaging are two standards that address the issues of reliable messaging. Both these standards are now part of OASIS.

Policy

Service providers sometimes require service consumers to communicate with certain policies. As an example a service provider may require a Kerberos security token for accessing the service. These requirements are defined as *policy assertions.* A policy may consist of multiple assertions. WS-Policy standardizes how policies are to be communicated between service consumers and service providers.

Orchestration

As enterprises embark on service architecture, services can be used to integrate silos of data, applications and components. Integrating applications means that the process requirements, such as asynchronous communication, parallel processing, data transformation and compensation, must be standardized. Web Services Business Process Execution Language (WSBPEL) is an OASIS specification that addresses service orchestration, where business processes are created using a set of discrete services. WSBPEL is now part of OASIS.

Management

As the number of services and business processes exposed as services grow in the enterprise a management infrastructure that lets the system administrators manage the services running in a heterogeneous environment becomes important. Web Services for Distributed Management (WSDM) will specify that any service implemented according to WSDM will be manageable by a WSDM-compliant management solution.

Other QoS attributes such as coordination between partners and transactions involving multiple services are being addressed in the WS-Coordination and WS-Transaction specifications, respectively, which are OASIS efforts as well.

2.7   Benefits of SOA

While the SOA concept is fundamentally not new, SOA differs from existing distributed technologies in that most vendors accept it and have an application or platform suite that enables SOA. SOA, with a ubiquitous set of standards brings better reusability of existing assets or investments in the enterprise and lets you create applications that can be built on top of new and existing applications [101-110]. SOA enables changes to applications while keeping clients or service consumers isolated from evolutionary changes that happen in the service implementation. SOA enables upgrading individual services or services consumers; it is not necessary to completely rewrite an application or keep an existing system that no longer addresses the new business requirements. Finally, SOA provides enterprises better flexibility in building applications and business processes in an agile manner by leveraging existing application infrastructure to compose new services.

2.8   Futures of SOAP

Simple Object Access Protocol (SOAP) is a simple XML-based protocol to let applications exchange information over HTTP. At present, SOAP seems to be the technology of choice for Web services. It is a platform-independent, XML-based protocol for remote (or local) method invocation.

SOAP defines an XML-based framework for unidirectional message exchange, accommodating the use of either HTTP or the Simple Mail Transfer Protocol (SMTP) as the transport mechanism. SOAP defines a message encapsulation format that comprises an <Envelope>, any number of <Header>s, and a single <Body>. It also specifies rules for processing <Header>s at intermediate hops but restricts <Body> processing to the end receiver. The <Body>

contains the user's XML data, and the <Envelope> specifies the service to be invoked. The data in the <Body> must be in a structure that both the requesting and receiving parties understand [111-120].

Typically, those interfaces are described in WSDL and the requester has to make sure that the request conforms to the interface. SOAP also separately defines transport-layer bindings to specific frequently used protocols. Currently the only defined bindings are for HTTP and SMTP.

Services typically employ a request-and-response architecture. An HTTP session is inherently synchronous, as is the underlying TCP connection .The RPC-like transaction model is thus a natural extension of the synchronous, HTTP-based, SOAP messaging infrastructure. The requester will typically embed input data into a HTTP POST request and the service will respond with the data embedded in the HTTP response. SOAP also supports asynchronous messaging (through the use of Web service call backs), though they are less prevalent. In this case, the HTTP response would contain no data and the service would respond with an HTTP POST of its own, at some later time. This call-back architecture does require however that the client have an HTTP server and a valid callback service enabled.

2.8.1 SOAP Objectives

- SOAP stands for Simple Object Access Protocol
- SOAP is a communication protocol
- SOAP is for communication between applications
- SOAP is a format for sending messages
- SOAP communicates via Internet
- SOAP is platform independent
- SOAP is language independent
- SOAP is based on XML
- SOAP is simple and extensible
- SOAP allows you to get around firewalls

2.9 Why SOAP

It is important for application development to allow Internet communication between programs. Today's applications communicate using Remote Procedure Calls (RPC) between objects like DCOM and CORBA, but HTTP was not designed for this. RPC represents a compatibility and security problem; firewalls and proxy servers will normally block this kind of traffic. A better way to communicate between applications is over HTTP, because HTTP is supported by all Internet browsers and servers. SOAP was created to accomplish this. SOAP provides a way to communicate between applications running on different operating systems, with different technologies and programming languages [121-130].

2.9.1   SOAP Building Blocks

A SOAP message is an ordinary XML document containing the following elements:

- An Envelope element that identifies the XML document as a SOAP message.
- A Header element that contains header information.
- A Body element that contains call and response information.
- A Fault element containing errors and status information.

2.9.2   Syntax Rules

Here are some important syntax rules:

- A SOAP message MUST be encoded using XML.
- A SOAP message MUST use the SOAP Envelope namespace.
- A SOAP message MUST use the SOAP Encoding namespace.
- A SOAP message must NOT contain a *Document Type Definition* (DTD) reference.
- A SOAP message must NOT contain XML Processing Instructions.

What are web services?

A web service is a software system designed to support interoperable machine-to-machine interaction over a network. It has an interface described in a machine-process able format (specifically WSDL). Other systems interact with the web service in a manner prescribed by its description using SOAP messages, typically conveyed using HTTP with an XML serialization in conjunction with other Web-related standards."

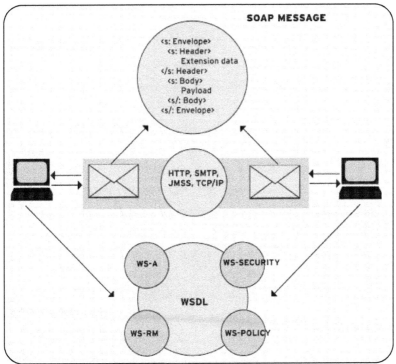

Figure 2.15: Simple Object access Protocol Architecture

Web service specifications are open, XML-based standards that are agreed upon through industry-wide participation in standard bodies like W3C or OASIS [131-140]. Figure 2.15 describes the SOAP Architecture, the architecture section will describe what these specifications are and how they all fit together to form the big picture.

2.10   The Web Services Architecture

Let's look at the web services architecture more closely. The Figure 2.15 depicts the layered architecture of the web services stack. Brief descriptions of each layer along with the relevant specifications are provided below. These specifications are very broad and discussing them in detail is outside the scope of this research. The purpose of the research is more or less to introduce them and describe what value each adds to the web services stack.

2.10.1 Transport Layer

The transport layer is responsible for carrying the SOAP message. As pointed out previously, web services are transport agnostic and web services stacks like Apache Axis2 support several transports.

2.10.2 Messaging Layer

SOAP is a specification defined by W3C. It is the fundamental messaging framework for web services. An important point to note is that from SOAP 1.2 and on, it is no longer an acronym. SOAP supports both document-literal and RPC programming models. A SOAP message consists of a single envelope and contains zero or more headers. The SOAP body contains business information commonly referred to as the payload. The SOAP specification does not define the actual contents of these headers or of the payload, but rather how it should be processed. The content is determined by the application that produces the SOAP message. Another important point is that, while the SOAP body is mandatory, the SOAP headers are optional. If an error is encountered while processing a SOAP message, it will result in a SOAP fault.

The optional SOAP headers provide the extensibility of the SOAP messaging structure. By specifying new headers you could compose new specifications based on SOAP. For example WS-Addressing is specified by defining new SOAP headers.

WS-Addressing provides transport-neutral mechanisms to address web services and messages. It defines the concept of an "endpoint reference," which encapsulates all the information that is required to reach a service endpoint at runtime. The value of WS-Addressing is that it provides a uniform way of identifying addressing information--such as where the message is going, where to return the response, or where to return an error without having to rely on the underlying transport mechanism. This also gives a standard way of routing messages over multiple transports. For example, a message could be sent for placing a purchase order over HTTP and after fulfilling the order the response can be sent over email (SMTP).

2.10.3 Description Layer

Web Services Description Language (WSDL) describes what your service is and how and where to access a service implementation. It is basically a contract between a service implementer and a service requester. A WSDL document defines two distinct parts. First, there is an abstract, reusable, implementation-independent section which describes the Service Interface. Then there's a concrete service-implementation description where the service is located. With WSDL comes the topic of Message Exchange Patterns, commonly referred to as MEPs. This topic will be discussed in a separate article.

WS-Policy provides important information about your web service which is not captured within a WSDL. It defines a general framework that can be used and extended by other web services specifications to describe a broad range of web services policies. WS-Policy defines a policy as a set of valid "policy alternatives." A policy alternative is a combination of policy assertions, which are individual capabilities or requirements. An example would be the type of security tokens that a service is capable of processing. Operators are defined to work on these policy alternatives, such as "ExactlyOne," "OneOrMore," and "ALL." Together they form a powerful framework to help two web services exchange configuration information at runtime to ensure their interoperability.

2.10.4 Quality of Service Layer

WS-Security family of specifications addresses the all-important aspect of security. These specifications ensure the authenticity, integrity and confidentiality of the SOAP messages. WS-Trust defines extensions that build on WS-Security to provide a framework for requesting and issuing security tokens and to broker trust relationships. WS-Secure Conversation builds on WS-Security and WS-Trust to provide secure communication across one or more messages.

WS-RM (Reliable Messaging) provides a specification to guarantee delivery and ordering of messages. This is archived via the concept of a Sequence and Sequence Acknowledgment. It defines semantics such as "AtMostOnce," "AtLeastOnce" and "InOrder." This is an important specification that adds reliability to your web services.

WS-Coordination provides a framework for coordinating the outcome between inter-operating web services. WS-Atomic Transactions and WS-Business Activity specify atomic and business transaction protocols that can be used with WS-Coordination. These specifications provide transaction support to web services to guarantee reliable and agreeable outcomes in distributed applications.

2.10.5 Component Layer

The layers below the component layer can be regarded as the infrastructure. The component layer consists of the web services (components) created by the application developer that capture the business logic. These components could be atomic or composite. WS-BPEL (Business Process Execution Language) is an extensible work-flow language that aggregates services by choreographing service interactions. In simpler terms, it's a model for defining how individual web services can collaborate together to create more complex and reliable business processes.

2.11 Applicability of Web Services

It is important to note that web services are not the magic cure for all problems. The technology has its own advantages and disadvantages that have to be carefully factored when determining the applicability of web services as a solution to a given problem. Below are some general guidelines, but remember that these are only general recommendations. Common sense should prevail, as it should with most situations where there is no rigid set of rules that can be used to determined applicability.

Do you operate in a homogeneous environment where your applications are static and mostly standalone? If that's the case, then the investment of taking a web services approach may not yield significant benefits. Is your application very sensitive to response times? If so, web services may not be an appropriate choice. Processing of XML messages is both time- and memory-intensive.

Is your application designed with the intention of supporting/communicating with various partners/customers that are not yet clearly identified? If so, a web services approach may reap rich benefits because you don't know the target platform, vendors, or technologies your intending partners or customers use. The web services approach will help you provide a technology- and platform-independent interface for your prospective partners or customers.

2.12   Engaging a Web Service

There are many ways that a requester entity might engage and use a Web service. In general, the following broad steps are required, as illustrated in Figure 2.16 the requester and provider entities become known to each other (or at least one becomes know to the other) the requester and provider entities somehow agree on the service description and semantics that will govern the interaction between the requester and provider agents the service description and semantics are realized by the requester and provider agents and the requester and provider agents exchange messages, thus performing some task on behalf of the requester and provider entities. (I.e., the exchange of messages with the provider agent represents the concrete manifestation of interacting with the provider entity's Web service.)

A Web service is a method of communication between two electronic devices over a network. "Web service" as "a software system designed to support interoperable machine-to-machine interaction over a network [144]. It has an interface described in a machine-processsble format (specifically Web Services Description Language, known by the acronym WSDL). Other systems interact with the Web service in a manner prescribed by its description using SOAP messages, typically conveyed using HTTP with an XML serialization in conjunction with other Web-related standards."

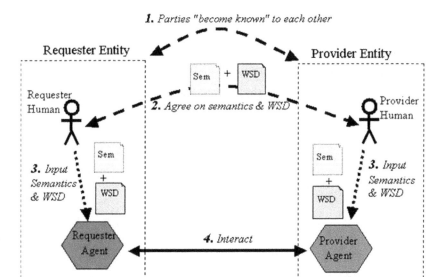

Figure 2.16: The General Process of Engaging a Web Service

2.13   Summary

As the number of online document collections increase and the number of users accessing these collections increase, it will be necessary to develop efficient distributed IR systems to access these collections. Distributed IR systems present unique problems to designers of distributed system due to the types of operations performed.

We present the implementation of a prototype distributed information retrieval system. The prototype is based on SOA, an existing and effective standalone IR system. We developed a detailed simulation model to test the performance of the distributed system under varying parameters and configurations. The simulator provides an easy and flexible platform for quickly performing different experiments in a controlled environment. To accurately model the actual system, the simulator uses many measurements obtained from the prototype system.

We present a series of experiments using the simulator to analyze the performance of the distributed IR architecture. We designed the experiments to test system utilization and identify potential bottlenecks under different workloads and system configurations. The experiments vary many parameters including the number of clients and web servers, terms per query, distribution of terms in queries, and the number of documents retrieved.

The major conclusions derived from the present study are as follows. Approach and implementation of information querying retrieval system can be used for querying and analysis with each module being loosely coupled with other. Following the summary of results achieved. The following models are implemented in the subsequent chapters.

1. Context independent and configurable module design.
2. Service oriented model design where each module behaves independent of each other.
3. Generic modules to perform querying and analysis on an underlying relational database.
4. Dynamic query interface module which can be plugged in to any web based program to interact with system.

CHAPTER - 3

IMPLEMENTING SOA FOR INFORMATION RETRIEVAL

3.1   Background

At the core of service-oriented architectures (SOAs) are distributed software components provided or accessed by independent third parties. Because access is not limited to a specific organization, explicit component contracts and universally adopted standards must support third-party access. Although such contracts could cover any technical or business aspects of service interaction, the current focus is on quality-of-service (QoS) policies. From SOA point of view, must be consider two separate aspects of the use of QoS policies: interoperability between components, which is the subject of the Web services specifications stack; and composition, which composition models, such as the Service Component Architecture (SCA), specifies the, "Components, Services, and Contracts" sidebar describes, a service contract covers both functional and nonfunctional aspects of a service component's visible behavior.

3.2   Related Work

Functional aspects are the component operations business semantics, including the business interface and protocol components as follows. Nonfunctional aspects include the interaction's technical features, such as data serialization and QoS protocols (reliable messaging and confidentiality). They can also include higher business-level characteristics that are not intrinsic to the service interaction, such as legal requirements. Standards and infrastructure are widely available to support the most basic form of SOA contracts: Functional interfaces are encoded using descriptions in the web services description language, which has been designed to support the inclusion of policies and semantic information. Policies encode QoS properties such as security, reliable delivery and transactional behavior.

SOA contracts based on these Web services standards are already becoming commonplace in enterprise and scientific computing. However, basic support is not enough, if the SOA concept is to achieve its full potential, the SOA framework must evolve toward richer and more meaningful contracts. To meet the respective objective, work is through industry specific standards to provide shared business semantic definitions across industries. There is significant growth in semantic Web services research to provide a more flexible support environment for such contracts. These two developments one to standardize industry specific semantics and the other to incorporate semantic capabilities into the basic infrastructure are complementary and could revolutionize the practice of SOA and enterprise computing. Central to these developments are the understanding of the web services specification stack supports nonfunctional contracts as policies and how policies in turn affect service composition.

3.3   Implementing the SOA Concepts

A service-oriented architecture is essentially a collection of services. These services communicate with each other. The communication can involve either simple data passing or it could involve two or more services coordinating some activity, while connecting services to each other is needed.

Service-oriented architectures are not a new idea for many users during last applications. At present these SOA technically specified the use of Distributed Component Object Model (DCOM) or Object Request Brokers (ORBs) based on the CORBA specification.

3.3.1   Client Server Connections

The technology of Web services are the most likely connection oriented technology of service-oriented architectures. Web services essentially use XML to create a robust connection.

As mentioned in Figure 3.1 shows a service consumer at the right sending a service request message to a service provider at the left. The service provider returns a response message to the service consumer. The request and subsequent response connections are defined in some way that is understandable to both the service consumer and service provider. How those connections are defined is explained in Web Services explained. A service provider can also be a service consumer.

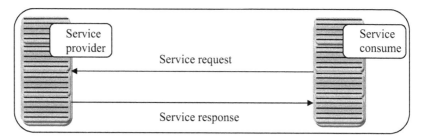

Figure 3.1: Primitive Service-Oriented Architecture

The concept of a service is nothing new, but the perception of an SOA has evolved over the past couple of years. It's an architectural style of building software applications that promotes loose coupling between components so that user can reuse them. Because it is a new way of building applications with the following characteristics:

- Services are software components that have published contracts/interfaces these contracts are platform, language and operating system independent. XML and the Simple Object Access Protocol (SOAP) are the enabling technologies for SOA, since they're platform-independent standards.
- Consumers can dynamically discover services.
- Services are interoperable.

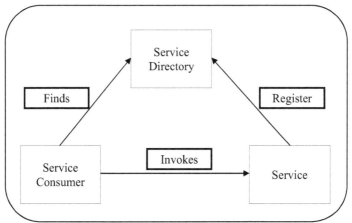

Figure 3.2: Service-Oriented Architecture

As mentioned in the above Figure 3.2 the basic building block of SOA is the service. A service is a self-contained software module that performs a predetermined task: "verify a customer's credit history," for example. Services are software components that don't require developers to use a specific underlying technology. As Java developers, tends to focus on reusing code, which tends to tightly integrate the logic of objects or components within an application. However, SOA promotes application assembly because services can be reused by numerous consumers. For example, in order to create a service that charges a consumer's credit card, we build and deploy only one instance of such a service; then we can consume this service from any number of applications.

The important key advantage of SOA is business-process management. Business processes may consume and orchestrate these services to achieve the desired functionality. The new business processes can be constructed by using existing services. For example, a customer order that has been submitted to shipping can be represented by a business process that can asynchronously interact with the requisite services.

3.4   Generic Information Retrieval System

In principle with SOA approach we have developed web services modules which can communicate with the clients and exchange information. We have used Apache axis2 engine for developing the web services. Two type of service model were developed which can be used by the clients programs. They are AXIOM and ADB. Approach for develop a generic client module to communicate with services. Figure 3.3 shows the Information Exchange with Generic Query Retrieval System.

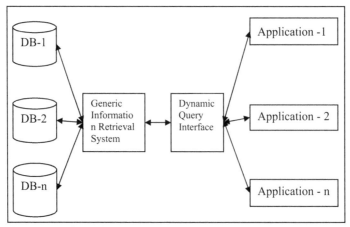

Figure 3.3: Information Exchange with Generic Query Retrieval System

3.4.1 AXIOM (Axis2 Object Model) Method

Since XML is the universally accepted method of information exchange apache axis2 provides XML object model for efficient SOAP messaging. Instead of the XML Axiom data object becomes the method of data transfer. It supports a novel "pull-through" model which allows one to turn off the tree building and directly access the underlying pull event stream. It also has built in support for XML Optimized Packaging (XOP) and MTOM, the combination of which allows XML to carry binary data efficiently and in a transparent manner. Since the nature of message transfer will be both in and out we have to define appropriate message receiver in the Service.xml file.

After receiving the Input AXIOM the web services will process the AXIOM and return the appropriate xml file as an AXIOM model. Typical input AXIOM can look like Figure 3.4.

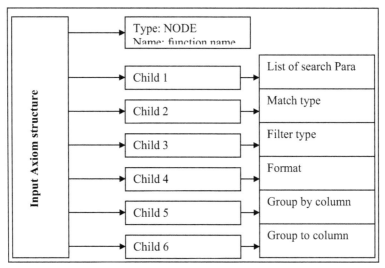

Figure 3.4: AXIOM Object Model

3.4.2   ADB (Axis2 Data Binding) Method.

This model is the most advance model which provides the application to send and receive java object instead of the Axiom which they can directly use in the application. The ADB framework provides a linking code from the WSDL file which can be directly used by the applications. From the WSDL file skeleton code can be generated where later we can put the business logic from the existing java code. Connecting code is created by the wsdl4java library. Based on the WSDL the wsdl2java API creates the connecting code which is called the stub code also. Following block Diagram shows the basic information flow of the ADB server model.

3.5   Technologies for Efficient Data Integration

To efficiently integrate semantically heterogeneous information from multiple data sources, Information Retrieval uses several technologies.

- Machine-learning techniques for converting traditional legacy Web sources and databases into Web services.
- A record linkage system for integrating data from multiple sources referring to a single entity.
- A mediator system providing uniform access to data from various Web services.
- An efficient execution system for information- gathering agents.
- Resource Description Framework (RDF) and *RDF Data Query Language (*RDQL) formalisms for representing queries and query results.

General systems usually consist of several subsystems which are working together towards its aims. Integration is a process by which smaller pieces of software or systems are brought together to form a larger piece of software or system that was designed to solve a problem or perform a comprehensive application. There are two architectures for integrating applications. The first is the point to point architecture and the other is the architectures based on middleware. The point to point method is fast, simple and suitable for small scale of system integration. On the other hand, if the number of modules and subsystems increase the stability of integrated system decreases. To overcome of this weakness a middleware layer is needed. Using this middleware a general interface is created to reduce the dependency of applications and let them to communicate through messages.

The integration layer can interact with the business logic layer through application or service interfaces. This pattern can be very effective in the right circumstances. There are different kinds of functional integration.

3.5.1 Message-Oriented Middleware Integration

It connects systems by using asynchronous message queues that are based on proprietary message-oriented middleware. Delivery process can be done even if sender and receiver of messages be not available or active because the communication is asynchronous and stable; there is little chance that the messages will be lost during a network or system failure. So this mechanism provides a way for communication between heterogeneous and different application. RPC is a sample of this service.

3.5.2 Distributed Object Integration

Building a distributed system is much more complicated than a centralized one. Developing separate components for any application is caused heterogeneous in programming language and platform. In addition, if we distribute the component of application on network, we will have many challenges such as: management of locating components, asynchronous communication between components, control and security. In fact, challenges are made between operating system and application developer for solving mentioned problems. Distributed object middleware is a layer between distributed applications and operating system for solving problems. Distributed object integration extends the model of object oriented computing to distributed solutions. Objects in an application interact with objects in another application. It means they would interact locally with other objects. Message oriented middleware connects systems by using asynchronous message queues that are based on proprietary message oriented middleware. CORBA and Remote Method Invocation (RMI) are samples of this middleware.

3.5.3 Service-Oriented Integration

Service oriented integration connects systems by enabling them to consume and provide XML Web services. Service integration enables interoperability and permits integration of heterogeneous components. SOA1 is a design philosophy that treats integration as the primary design principle rather than as an afterthought. The architecture is called service-oriented because applications and functions appear as a loosely coupled set of services. A "service" in SOA is an application or function with well-defined interfaces that is packaged as a reusable component for use in a business process. Simply stated, in an SOA, business processes appear as a set of separate components that can be joined and choreographed to create composite applications and processes. Selecting the appropriate integration method is suited to desired application in integration system. Proposed work emphasis on information retrieval system and has been tried to select an appropriate method with considering special needs of information retrieval system. The characteristic like ease of scalability and fast responding to user query are very important in IR systems. So, in order to ease scalability of integration system in future, low complexity of implementation and high interoperability are important. Because people have different knowledge and expertise, another important feature that is related to user is simplified of implementation. For example distributed object integration like CORBA has fast responding time but it has very complex implementation. Contrary, service oriented approach has low complex implementation. On the other hand the study shows that the popular search engine such as Yahoo and Google works by web service. So according to mentioned reasons and the importance degree of selected indices for our application the web service is a suitable technology for our integration framework.

3.6 Information Retrieval using Web Services

Apache axis2 is used as the web service platform along with Apache Tomcat .The web services model is described in the Figure 3.5.

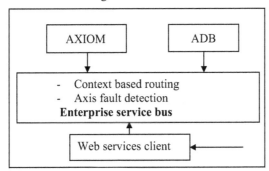

Figure 3.5: Web Service System

XML format was preferred over the traditional delimiter separated file because of the ability of xml to show the hierarchical relations in an effective manner and also due to the flexibility to make changes without affecting the existing structure. An XML schema was design to represent the tables in a database and also the relations between the tables. Also we have tried to address the issue of heterogeneity in terms of column naming etc. Following block diagram shows the design of the schema search column refers to the columns of the table available for searching, display column refers to the column data to be displayed in case of table specific data display. The synonym list section contains more than one synonym block which is for displaying the relations between tables. Each synonym block has a primary column element which refers to the columns which are related to other tables, second column element are column name which are present in other tables but with a different nomenclature or in other words the related column to the primary column in other tables.

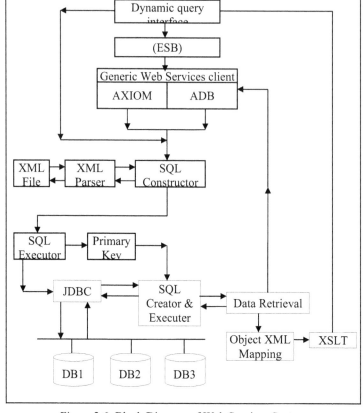

Figure 3.6: Block Diagram of Web Services System

The block diagram of SOA approach for information retrieval system using web services system is shown in Figure 3.6 and it is implemented using java platform. The XML parsing and Extensible Style sheet Language (XSLT) transformation is implemented using Apache Xerec and Xalan API. Object XML mapping was implemented with Castor API. The query interpreter processes the input search data.

The SQL query creator perform the process of finding table info of the search columns and forming SQL queries and then the SQL query executer performs execution and storing required key value pair as discussed in the implementation part. After the primary key retrieval, data is retrieved based on the method selected .If no global xml data is presents then data is stored in data objects. Based on the client's request the data is converted to xml using Object xml mapping concepts using Castor API or converted to Hyper Text Markup Language (HTML) using XSLT transformation on the output of above step or converted to the AXIOM model and transmitted else data object itself is transmitted.

3.7   Combining Semantic Web and IR Using Web Services

Semantic web will provide intelligent access to heterogeneous, distributed information, enabling software products to mediate between user needs and the information sources available. Web services can be accessed and executed via the web. However, all these service descriptions are based on semi-formal natural language descriptions. Therefore, the human programmer needs to be kept in the loop and the scalability as well as economy of web services is limited. Bringing them to their full potential requires their combination with semantic web technology. This technology will provide mechanization in service identification, configuration, comparison and combination. Semantic web enabled web services have the potential to change our life to a much higher degree than the current web already has. Semantic retrieval to support web services will be the promising vision in the foreseeable future.

3.7.1   Semantic Information Retrieval

The system first assigns a syntactic analysis to input from either a query or document. At the heart of the approach is a mapping of this structure to concepts in the UMLS domain model. The most important information which is then available for further analysis is a semantic type for each concept which is situated in a network of such types. Further semantic processing constructs a predicate argument structure which determines how the concepts discovered in the previous phase interact within a particular linguistic structure. For example, in slightly simplified form, our syntactic component assigns the underspecified structure (1b) to the input (1a). Thermogram and meningitis map to the UMLS concepts shown in (1c), which is the semantic interpretation for this example and provides both the UMLS concepts as well as the associated semantic types. The semantic interpretation specifies the relationship which obtains between the concepts in the input phrase.

(1)   a. Use of thermogram in detection of meningitis.

        b. noun_phrase([head(use)],
              [prep(of), head(thermogram)],
              [prep(in), head(detection)]
              [prep(of), head(meningitis)])

        c. detection(
              theme(head(meningitis,
              concept("Meningitis"),
              semtype('Disease or Syndrome'))), instr(head(thermogram,
              concept("Thermography"),
              semtype('Diagnostic Procedure'))))

We have a running prototype which produces underspecified syntactic analysis, successfully maps noun phrases to the UMLS domain model, and then builds semantic structures.

3.7.2 Mapping Phrases in Free Text to the UMLS Metathesaurus

We have attempted to combine the most effective aspects of the various approaches to using phrases in information retrieval. Our system first identifies phrases in free text using an underspecified syntactic analysis. We claim that such an approach supports the semantic representations which can effect accurate matching of queries to relevant documents but avoids the problems associated with a fully specified syntactic analysis as noted, for example, by Salton and Smith. Our syntactic component is closely allied to work in underspecified syntactic analysis of the type discussed in and similar in depth of coverage to the work. We begin by analyzing noun phrases and prepositional phrases. In a successful syntactic analysis, heads are identified and most items to the left of the head are simply labeled as "modifier"; however, participles are singled out and labeled as such. Prepositional phrases are implicitly identified, but during the syntactic phase their attachment is not indicated. Although the syntactic structure we produce is not fully specified, it has advantages over the unstructured phrases obtained from a barrier word approach. Most importantly, the identification of heads of noun phrases has significant consequences during the mapping of such phrases to concepts in the Metathesaurus, as will be seen in the following section. An example of the type of syntactic structure we assign is given in (2b) for the input in (2a).

2)   a. patients with sustained ventricular tachycardia treated with amiodarone

       b. noun_phrase([[head(patients)],

           [prep(with),mod(sustained),mod(ventricular),

           head(tachycardia),pastpart(treated)],

           [prep(with),head(amiodarone)]]])

Note in this example the structure is extremely flat; very little commitment is made to the internal structure of the noun phrase. For example, the past participle treated is not assigned a syntactic structure which directly reflects its final interpretation. At the same time, the fact that tachycardia is labeled as a head and distinguished from treated has important consequences during subsequent processing. We claim that the structural information provided by this analysis contains the optimal amount of information for further processing, namely the mapping of simple noun phrases to concepts in UMLS and the construction of a semantic interpretation. After all noun phrases have been identified, we map these structures to concepts in the Metathesaurus using a comprehensive mapping program which employs extensive variant generation as well as a principled way of dealing with partial matches between the phrase and Metathesaurus concepts. Variant generation is determined by the information available from our lexicon and associated knowledge bases. Variants are recursively computed by generating morphological variants, synonyms, acronyms and abbreviations for each lexical word in the input phrase. For example, all variants for the phrase ocular complications are listed in (3).

(3)   ocular, oculars, oculus, oculi, eyepiece,

eyepieces, eye, eyes, eyed, eyeing, eying, optic,

optics, optical, optically, vision, ophthalmic,

opthalmia, ophthalmiac, ophthalmiacs,

complication, complications.

Once variants have been generated for a given phrase, candidate terms from the Metathesaurus are identified. Such candidates for a noun phrase consist of the set of all Metathesaurus terms which contain at least one of the variants computed for the phrase and which satisfy a further condition on partial matches discussed below. The candidates for ocular complications appear in (4), where preferred terms are given in parentheses.

(4)   "Complications" ("Complication")

"complications <1>"

"Eye"

"Optic" ("Optics")

"Ophthalmia" ("Endophthalmitis")

"Vision"

The final step in the mapping process combines the best candidates to form mappings between the noun phrase and one or more Metathesaurus terms. The degree of similarity between a noun phrase and a Metathesaurus concept is based on factors which take into account how much variation is used to accomplish the match, whether the head is involved, and how much of the Metathesaurus concept and the noun phrase are involved in the match. This last criterion is based on various types of matches which can occur between a noun phrase and a Metathesaurus term. In a simple match the noun phrase maps to a single Metathesaurus term. For example, the input phrase intensive care unit maps to "Intensive Care Units". In a complex match there is a partitioning of the noun phrase so that each element of the partition has a simple match to a term in the Metathesaurus. Thus, intensive care medicine maps to the two terms "Intensive Care" and "Medicine". In a partial match the noun phrase maps to a Metathesaurus term in such a way that at least one word of either the noun phrase or the Metathesaurus term (or both) does not participate in the mapping. Some examples of partial matches are given in (5).

(5)   liquid crystal thermography maps to

"Thermography"

ambulatory monitoring maps to "Ambulatory Electrocardiographic Monitoring"

obstructive sleep apnea maps to "Obstructive Apnea"

We eliminate partial matches in which both the first and last words of the Metathesaurus term do not participate in the match. This allows ambulatory monitoring to map to the Metathesaurus term "Ambulatory Electrocardiographic Monitoring" above, but disallows, for example, left ventricle from mapping to the term "Left Ventricular Outflow Obstruction". With regard to the phrase ocular complications, this rule eliminates "Postoperative Complications". Mappings which do not satisfy this rule do not constitute the best mapping between noun phrase and Metathesaurus. In the final determination of the mappings between noun phrase and Metathesaurus term, both less variation and involvement of the head contribute to a stronger match. In general, a simple match represents a stronger mapping between the input phrase and the Metathesaurus term, while complex matches are less strong, and partial matches represent the weakest mapping from input to Metathesaurus. These criteria determine that of the candidate Metathesaurus terms given in (4), those listed in (6) constitute the best map to ocular complications.

(6)   "Eye"

       "Complication", "complications <1>"

3.7.3   Relationships between Phrases: Semantic Processing

Semantic interpretation indicates dependencies among the concepts identified by mapping noun phrases to concepts in the Metathesaurus. We represent these dependencies in a predicate argument structure that we call conceptual structure, which is closely related to logical form. The arguments in conceptual structure are labeled with semantic case roles in order to more clearly specify the relationships among the concepts represented. For example, we construct the (simplified) conceptual structure given in (7) to represent the semantic interpretation of hemofiltration in digoxin overdose. The case labels on the arguments in (7) indicate that it is digoxin overdose that is being treated through the use of hemofiltration as an instrument.

(7)   treat(theme(digoxin overdose),

       instr(hemofiltration))

Conceptual structures are built through the application of semantic rules which fall into two major categories. As much as possible we rely on the UMLS Semantic Network since doing so diminishes the number of semantic rules we must write. When application of the Semantic Network is not possible, we appeal to rules which depend crucially on the semantic types obtained from UMLS and which are similar in spirit to those discussed in. In exploiting the Semantic Network for semantic interpretation we match linguistic patterns against corresponding relationships between semantic types in the Network. As an example, consider the text single corticospinal axons in the cat spinal cord and note that axons has semantic type 'Cell Component', while spinal cord is of type 'Body Part, Organ, or Organ Component'. Furthermore, in the Semantic Network these two semantic types are joined by the relation 'part_of' as noted in (8).

(8)   part_of('Cell Component',

        'Body Part, Organ, or Organ Component')

In order to exploit these facts for semantic interpretation we need only stipulate that the preposition in may correspond to the Semantic Network relation 'part_of'. Then, since single corticospinal axons in the cat spinal cord contains the preposition in and since its semantic types correspond to those in (8) this relationship provides the semantic interpretation (9).

(9)   part_of(nom(single corticospinal axons),theme(cat spinal cord))

For situations in which an interpretation based on the Semantic Network does not apply, we supply rules of semantic interpretation, which crucially depend on the UMLS semantic types. In this regard, the semantic types associated with Metathesaurus concepts can be generalized. For example, frostbite has the semantic type 'Injury or Poisoning', while malaria is typed as 'Disease or Syndrome'. We collapse these types and others referring to medically treatable conditions into the generalized type <disorder>. An example of a domain-specific semantic rule is (10), which states that a noun phrase which is the object of the preposition for and whose head has any of the UMLS semantic types covered by the generalized semantic type <disorder> can modify a minimal noun phrase to the left whose head has the semantic type <therapy>. Furthermore, the rule states that in conceptual structure the relationship between the noun phrases is such that the therapy is used as an instrument to treat the disorder. Rule (10) applies to (11a) to produce (11b).

(10)   [head(<therapy>)] ,[prep(for), head(<disorder>)]

        treat(theme(<disorder>),instr(<therapy>))

(11)   a. Electrocoagulation for gastrointestinal hemorrhage.

        b. treat(theme(gastrointestinal hemorrhage), instr(electrocoagulation))

3.7.4   Exploiting Semantic Structure for Information Retrieval

In conclusion, we suggest a method of exploiting semantic structure to improve retrieval effectiveness. The example in (12) is constructed to be paradigmatic of one problem associated with the use of either key words or phrases in information retrieval. Title (12b) is relevant to query (12a) while (12c) is not.

(12)   a. Query: Intra-carotid injection of drugs for the treatment of malignant

            gliomas

        b. Title1: Intra-carotid BCNU chemotherapy for malignant gliomas

        c. Title2: Association of internal carotid aneurysms and temporal glioma

A reasonable translation of (12a) into a Boolean query might be (carotid AND glioma). It is not advisable to include injection in the Boolean query, since the concept represented by intra-carotid injection could well be represented in text by some form of infusion, perfusion, or chemotherapy, at least. Given this query it is not possible to reject the non relevant (12c). The use of phrases does not solve the problem, and in fact makes it worse. The Boolean translation of the query using phrases would probably be (intra-carotid injections AND gliomas). This rejects the non relevant title, but also rejects the relevant title. The use of terms from the Metathesaurus alone also does not help. "Injections" (the term for intra-carotid injection) does not match "Chemotherapy" (the term for intra-carotid BCNU chemotherapy). A solution based on semantic processing depends on the partial (and simplified) conceptual structures for the query and texts given in (13).

(13) a. treat(theme(malignant gliomas),

instr(intra-carotid injection))

b. treat(theme(malignant gliomas),

instr(intra-carotid BCNU chemotherapy))

c. co-occurs_with(

cotheme(internal carotid aneurysm),

cotheme(temporal glioma))

The most important aspect of (13) relevant to the problem under discussion is that the query and the relevant title involve the predicate treat. In (13a) and (13b) a concept with the semantic type 'Disease or Syndrome' is treated by a concept with semantic type 'Therapeutic or Preventive Procedure'. A quite different semantic structure has been assigned to the non relevant title (13c), in which a 'Disease or Syndrome' co-occurs with an 'Acquired Abnormality'. These facts based on semantic conceptual structure can be used to improve retrieval precision by including a stipulation on the retrieval mechanism which states that in order for a query to match text, the main predicate in the semantic structure of the query must match the main predicate in the conceptual structure of the text. This requirement eliminates the non relevant title (13c) above as a possible match to the query. Once such a requirement has been met, the normal Boolean query can be issued to retrieve the relevant title (13b). In so far as semantics is able to identify relationships between phrases and thus more precisely represent the content of text, we see this type of processing as showing considerable promise for being able to enhance existing information retrieval techniques based on phrases, whether the phrases are directly identified in text or result from mapping to a controlled vocabulary.

3.8 Chapter Conclusion

- This chapter comprises implementation of the SOA for information retrieval. Service-oriented architecture is essentially a collection of services. These services communicate with each other. The communication can involve either simple data passing or it could involve two or more services coordinating some activity. Means of connecting services to each other is needed.

- Today's IT organizations invariably employ disparate systems and technologies. Most analysts predict that J2EE and .NET will continue to coexist in most organizations and the trend of having heterogeneous technologies in IT shops will continue. Moreover, creating applications that leverage these different technologies has historically been a daunting task.

- Services are the building blocks of service-oriented applications. Thus, services are somewhat analogous to Java objects and components such as EJBs. Unlike objects, however, services are self-contained, maintain their own state, and provide a loosely coupled interface.

- The models have been proposed in the following chapter to overcome the existing ones in information retrieval system.

- The full understanding of text is still an intangible goal. The scope of the Semantic Web is to translate current Web content into a format meaningful to computers. Several languages have been developed for this purpose, including XML, RDF, DAML, OIL, SHOE and others. The proposed work having Word Semantics model, which is simpler than XML or RDF, but it comes with the scope of advantages are feasible with existing technologies and resources.

- Practically, these new models relies on understanding word meanings, identifying important named entities such as person, organization and others, and linking all this information via an external general purpose SOA Architecture.

- With these features, developed model as a fair but strong step towards the long term goals of creating a SOA for information Retrieval which is implemented in the coming chapters.

CHAPTER - 4

METHODOLOGIES OF INFORMATION RETRIEVAL SYSTEM MODELS

The present research work involves information query retrieval system, the system can be decomposed to following modules which need to be worked upon to create a loosely coupled system.

1. Model to represent the underlying relational database in a generic form.

2. Model to represent the input query.

3. Model to generate queries based on input conditions and querying, filtering, grouping across databases based on the input query and dispatch the output.

4. Model to design the service interface to communicate with client application.

4.1 Model for Relational Database Representation in XML Format

XML format was preferred over the traditional delimiter separated file because of the ability of XML to show the hierarchical relations in an effective manner and also due to the flexibility to make changes without affecting the existing structure. XML schema was design to represent the tables in a database and also the relations between the tables. The implementation issues of heterogeneity in terms of column naming like searchcolumlist and synonyms. Following block diagram shows the design of the schema search column refers to the table available for searching and display column refers to the column data to be displayed in case of table specific data display. The synonym list section contains more than one synonym block which is for displaying the relations between tables. Each synonym block has a primary column element which refers to the columns which are related to other tables. Second column element are column name which are present in other tables but with a different classification, and each column having its own attributes of XML Schema representation as mention in the below Figure 4.1.

A relational database consists of a set of *tables,* where each table is a set of *records*. A record in turn is a set of *fields* and each field is a pair *field-name/field-value*. All records in a particular table have the same number of fields with the same field-names. The relational data-model also defines certain constraints on the tables and defines operations on them. We are not concerned with the constraints and operations here. In other words, we are not trying to create a query language or a data-definition language, just a language that captures the data in a database or in a particular view of the database. Here is an example of a single database with two tables.

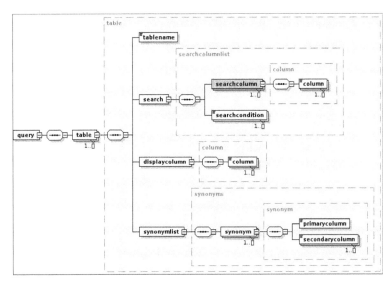

Figure 4.1: XML schema showing XML representation of relational database

<!doctype mydata " ">

<mydata>

<authors>

<author>

<name>Robert Roberts</name>

<address>10 Tenth St, Decapolis</address>

<editor>Ella Ellis</editor>

<ms type="blob">ftp://docs/rr-10</ms>

<born>1960/05/26</born>

</author>

<author>

<name>Tom Thomas</name>

<address>2 Second Av, Duo-Duo</address>

<editor>Ella Ellis</editor>

<ms type="blob">ftp://docs/tt-2</ms>

</author>

<author>

<name>Mark Marks</name>

<address>1 Premier, Maintown</address>

Ella Ellis

```
<ms type="blob">ftp://docs/mm-1</ms>
</author>
</authors>
<editors>
<editor>
<name>Ella Ellis</name>
<telephone>7356</telephone>
</editor>
</editors>
</mydata>
```

The format is verbose, since XML is verbose. On the other hand, it compresses well with standard compression tools. It is also easy to print the database (or a part of it) with standard XML browsers and a simple style sheet.

A relational can be modeled as a hierarchy of depth four: the database consists of a set of *tables,* which in turn consist of *records*, which in turn consist of *fields*. We can model the database with a <u>document node</u> and its associated <u>element node</u>:

```
<!doctype name "url">
<name>
table₁
table₂
...
tableₙ
</name>
```

The *name* is arbitrary. The *url* is optional, but can be used to point to information about the database. We don't define what it points to. The order of the tables is also arbitrary, since a relational database defines no ordering on them.

Each table of the database is represented by an <u>element node</u> with the records as its children:

```
<name>
record₁
record₂
...
recordₘ
</name>
```

The *name* is the name of the table. The order of the records is arbitrary, since the relational data model defines no ordering on them.

A record is also represented by an <u>element node</u>, with its fields as children:

    <name>

    field$_1$

    field$_2$

    ...

    field$_m$

    </name>

The *name* is arbitrary, since the relational data model doesn't define a name for a record type. However, in XML it cannot be omitted. One scheme is to re-use the name of the table, or, if the table has a name that is a plural, to use the singular form (`persons' -> `person', `parts' -> `part'). The order of the fields is again immaterial.

A field is represented as an <u>element node</u> with a <u>data node</u> as its only child:

    <name type="*t*">

    d

    </name

If *d* is omitted, it means the value of the fields is the empty string. The value of *t* indicates the type of the value (such as string, number, boolean, date). [Should we give a complete list?] If the type attribute is omitted, the type is assumed to be `string.' This model will allow an application that knows about these attributes to check the content of each field.

The flow of the model discussed elaborately step by step procedure and its results have been represented in subsequent chapter.

4.2 Model to Represent the Input Query

Input search query can either in a delimiter separated form or can be in XML form. Details are given below.

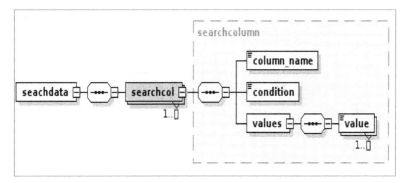

Figure 4.2: XML representation of input query

- Delimiter separated format
  - COLi = [cond]val1[::]@@@[cond]val2[::]... i =0 to n
- XML format is represented in Figure 4.2
- condition refers to condition like "!=","<" ,">" etc

HTML document does not contain structural information. In contrast, the XML document is far more easily accessible to machines because every piece of information is described in a structural form but it doesn't provide restrictions on the semantics of the data. As XML doesn't provide the semantics of the data Resource Description Framework (RDF) has been introduced which is a language for creating a data model for objects (resources) and relations between pairs of resources, providing a simple semantics for the data model. It represents date using labeled, directed graph of relations between resources and literal values, the graphs are collection of "triples". Triples are made up of a "subject (a resource)", a "predicate (property)" and an "object (property value)". The representation of input query is implemented by following methods.

4.2.1 Back-end Query Implementation

Query string by joining the relationships with the concept in reference to the unknown variable or entity. For example the user wants know that what the Cotton varieties cultivated in Central Karnataka is. Based on the given inputs the concepts are mapped to the below query.

> SELECT DISTINCT ?y
>
> WHERE
>
> {
>
>   ?Crop pl:hasCropName "Cotton"@en .
>
>   ?Crop pl:hasCropZone ?n.
>
>   ?n pl:CropZoneName "Central Karnataka"@en.
>
>   ?Crop pl:hasVariety ?y. }

Flow of execution of above query:

Crop⟶ CropName⟶ Cotton⟶ hasCropZone
(Concept) (Relationship) (Instance) (Relationship)

Y ⟵——————— hasVariety   Central_Karnataka
(Unknown entity)   (Relationship)   (Instance)

4.2.2 Logical Implementation of the back end module

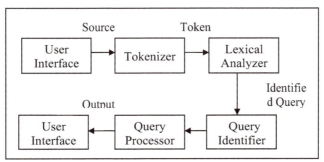

Figure 4.3: Block Representation of Back End Implementation

The implementation of the Back End module as shown in Figure 4.3 consists of three major components they are.

- **Keyword generation from the string entered by the user in simple English**

The source string entered by the user is tokenized by the Tokenizer and passed through a Lexical Analyzer. Here the tokens are compared to the keywords on the basis of match percentages already specified in the analyzer. The keywords and their respective percentage matches are stored and updated by the system administrator. This process will sift the relevant keywords from the input string. For example if user enters the following query "What are the Cotton varieties cultivated in Central Karnataka?". After tokenizing the above query by the Tokenizer the Lexical Analyzer identifies Cotton, varieties and Central Karnataka as the key words.

- **Query identification with the help of selected keywords**

The queries are stored against the largest number obtained by the indices of the keywords contained in the query. Thus the keyword indices obtained from the analyzer are arranged to form the largest possible number hence leading to the destination query.

- **Query processing**

The query identified through the above process is fired into the ontology and the results are returned to the user through a web interface.

4.2.3 Autosuggestion Feature for Taking Inputs from User

The user interface provided for the system requires the user to enter his query either in the form of certain concepts and relationships or as a sentence. This is achieved using the autosuggestion feature developed in Figure 4.4. For example, in the above query as soon as the user types a 'c' in the crop name input box, he is automatically suggested various crop names such as cotton, ground nut etc.

Figure 4.4: Index box for query input.

This model addresses the query execution time by rearranging the query by keeping the more specific part of the query first. The basic structures used in this model are:

1. Operators - They are depicted as nodes consisting of a head, a body and some additional annotations.

2. Dataflows - They are depicted as edges between the nodes. They act as connector which connects two operators and transfers the data provided by one of them and consumed by the other.

The proposed model implements the web service model need for a Semantic Web in various applications where we need to extract Information contextually. Thus the model aims to meet the growing need for Semantic web paradigm.

4.3 Model to Perform Querying and Filtering

Querying and filtering is design from the perspective of narrowing down on the most specific record based on the series input data. After Input condition is processed, for each search condition corresponding table details are retrieved and stored. Then for each table details queries are formed and data is retrieved. Each table query also has the output of previous query as a part of the condition thus relating to the previous table. There are two methods for filtering, they are 1.strict, 2.loose. Basic flow of query is given below.

- We start with the first input
- Second query will have output of the previous stage as condition in addition to the condition provided in the input query.

In the strict method the process of querying stops if no result id found at some stages, on the other hand in the loose method querying continues in the next table with output of previous stage where match was found as a condition in addition with the condition provided in the input query.

Algorithm

1. Process search string.
2. For 1 to n (n, no of search String)
3. Repeat step 3 and 4
4. Search column for table.

5. If table found, store table name, search column, search value and search condition
6. Initialize the result key value pair
7. For each stored table information in step4

    a) Check if result key value pair has any entry which is equal to the primary column of the current table

    b) If yes form the appropriate query

    c) Execute the query

    d) If strict option selected then

    e) Get the distinct value of primary column and store as key value pair replacing earlier keys if present with the new value.

    f) If no value found then empty the result key-value pair

        Else

Get the distinct value of primary column and store as key value pair replacing earlier keys if present with the new values.

8. After query of primary keys are obtained, data is retrieved

 a) If normal output

    If group by is enabled then

    If match is yes

        For each group by primary id

         For each match table make query

      Execute the query and store the data in appropriate objects

      Else

      If match is all

        For each group by group by primary id

         For each match table make query

       Execute the query store the data in appropriate object.

      Else

        For each table make query

      Execute the query store the data in appropriate object.

    Else

      Get the global xml from each primary key

The above algorithm limits the results of a database select query by using particular criteria. Our approach considers a document (or query) as constituted of conceptual components approximated as single terms and self-relevant to the document (query) itself, and we work in a universe consisting of document components rather than documents. Because of the self relevance assumption, every query (document) therefore has a relevant and irrelevant set even when no relevant judgment has been made, we are able to bootstrap and provide probabilistic weights to our terms at the initial retrieval stage. Because we work with conceptual components, repeat term usage and item lengths are accounted for, enabling us to remove the binary assumption restriction. The step no. 7 implements the familiar probabilistic query term weights but in the component environment. Step no. 8 is for document focused retrieval and the form of the weighting, after taking the approximation of all other frequencies, turns out to be very similar to those used via a language model approach.

The filtering and routing tasks were used as a test bed for our research in applying genetic algorithms leaning in Information Retrieval, in conjunction with the Probabilistic Information Retrieval. The results and comparison were discussed in the result analysis chapter 6.

Thus, our model may also be viewed as a combination of the probabilistic retrieval model and a simple language model. For many of the experiments, our system has been demonstrated to provide superior effectiveness.

4.4 Model to Perform Filtering and Grouping

Grouping is done with a prospective of classifying the output by a column which is referred as group by column. The important from statistical analysis, bar graph etc. Also it is very significant in domains like life science, finance. We have designed the model to perform a grouping operation between two column values not only in the same table but any tables in the system. After the filtering as described in the above step we have a series of key value pair as output. The details of group by and group to column are searched. Then for each value of group by column value subset of the output key-value pair is taken and then the corresponding group column is queried in the respective table of group column. So each group we obtain the data of group column which can be taken for next level of grouping.

a) Method1

Algorithm

1. Get cluster column

   Search for table info

   Get the output from step 6.

2. If cluster is done with specific values of cluster   column then make a count and group query on the group cluster table with output from step 6 and specified value of Custer column.

   Else

   Maker a count and group query on the group   cluster table with output from step 7 of querying algorithm.

b) Method2

1. Get cluster column x with value if any
2. Get cluster column y with value if any
3. Search table info of cluster x

   a. If cluster is to done with specific values of cluster column x then search specific values in respective table

      Else

      Get distinct value from specific table

   b. For each value of distinct cluster column x

   c. Create query from output from step 7 of querying algorithm.

4. Execute query for each value of cluster x column and

   Store the out as key value pair where key is the value of cluster x column and value is again a key value pair of output of query

5. Search for table information of cluster column y

   For each key value pair obtained in step 4

   a. Create and execute query

   b. Get the count for each value of cluster x column

6. Generate the XML output

An XML-based profile model needs efficient algorithms for structure and data filtering to achieve high performance in a large-scale environment such as the Internet. As a result, profile grouping and indexing are crucial for large scale XML document filtering. For this purpose, similar to traditional SDI systems, Filtering and Grouping Algorithm were designed. The method 1 is used to match documents to individual queries. Our implementation also allows for user profiles to be expressed as Boolean combinations of queries rather than being restricted to a single query. Such composite profiles are handled by post-processing the matching results at the Method 2 to check the Boolean conditions.

When a document arrives at the Filter Engine, it is run through an XML Parser which then drives the process of checking for matching profiles in the Index. We use an XML parser that is based on the SAX interface, which is a standard interface for *event-based* XML parsing. We developed the parser using the *expat* toolkit, which is a non-validating XML processor.

The SAX event-based interface reports parsing events (such as encountering the start or end tag of an element) directly to the application through callbacks, and does not usually build an internal tree. To use the SAX interface, the application must implement handlers to deal with the different events, much like handling events in a graphical user interface. For our application, we use the events to drive the profile matching process. Table 4.1 shows an example of how a SAX event-based interface breaks the structure of an XML document down into a linear sequence of events. For Filter, we implemented callback functions for the parsing events of encountering: 1) a begin element tag; 2) an end element tag; or 3) data internal to an element. All of the handlers are passed the name and document level of the element for (or in) which the parsing event occurred. Additional handler-specific information is also passed as described below.

An XML Document	SAX API Events
<?xml version="1.0">	start document, start element: doc
<doc>	start element: para
<para>	characters: Hello, world!
Hello, world!	end element: para
</para>	end element: doc
</doc>	end document

Table 4.1: SAX API Example

4.4.1 Start Element Handler

When an element tag is encountered by the parser, it calls this handler, passing in the name and level of the element encountered as well as any XML attributes and values that appear in the element tag. The handler looks up the element name in the Query Index and examines all the nodes in the Candidate List for that entry. For each node, it performs two checks: a level check and an attribute filter check. The purpose of the level check is to make sure that the element appears in the document at a level that matches the level expected by the query. If the path node contains a nonnegative level value, then the two levels must be identical in order for the check to succeed. Otherwise, the level for the node is unrestricted, so the check succeeds regardless of the element level. The attribute filter check applies any simple predicates that reference the attributes of the element. If both checks succeed and there are no other filters to be checked, then the node passes. If this is the final path node of the query (i.e., its final state) then the document is deemed to match the query. Otherwise, if it is not the final node, then the query is moved into its next state. This is done by copying the next node for the query from its Wait List to its corresponding Candidate List (note that a copy of the promoted node remains in the Wait List). If the RelativePos value of the copied node is not -1, its level value is also updated using the current level and its RelativePos values to do future level checks correctly.

4.4.2 End Element Handler

When an end element tag is encountered, the corresponding path node is deleted from the Candidate List in order to restore that list to the state it was in when the corresponding start element tag was encountered. This "backtracking" is necessary to handle the case where multiple elements with the same name appear at the different level in the document.

4.4.3 Element Characters Handler

This handler is called when the data associated with an element is encountered. The data is passed in to the handler as a parameter. It works similarly to the Start Element Handler except that it performs a content filter check rather than an attribute filter check. That is, it evaluates any filters that reference the element content. Like the Start Element Handler, this handler can also cause the query to move to its next state.

We have proposed this model to allow users to define their interests using the query language. This approach enables the construction of more expressive profiles than current IR-based profile models by exploiting the structural information available in XML documents. We developed indexing mechanisms and matching algorithms based on a modified Finite State Machine (FSM) approach that can quickly locate and evaluate relevant profiles.

4.5 Model to Design the Service Interface to Communicate With Clients.

Once the information retrieve methods were finalized, service interfaces were to be designed in order to communicate with other services. Following approaches were followed.

4.5.1 Web Based Dynamic Query Interface Based on the XML File Used to Showcase the Underlying Database.

Objective of the dynamic query interface was to provide a loosely coupled system which interacts with the information retrieval system .This can be used as a plug in any web based client server model.

User interface could be created by parsing the XML file representing the database systems (Figure 4.2) and creating the HTML input form based on the table and fields. Since web based tool depends on parameter passing for sending request which is again dependent on the name of the input elements in the Input form, we need to work on a generic nomenclature methodology to make the interface components context independent. Then a generic block to communicate with the services upon submitting the data on the user interface.

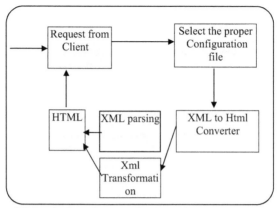

Figure 4.5: Basic flow diagrams for dynamic query interface process

Figure 4.5 shows the basic flow diagrams for dynamic query interface process based on the XML file used to showcase the underlying database.

Algorithm

1. gobal_counter =0
2. For each table
    a. Put the Table heading
    b. get all search columns
3. For each search columns
    a. Put the label as the column heading
    b. Create an input text element with "id"   having a   specific pattern
    c. pattern="search::"+gobal_counter
    d. <input type="text" id=pattern   value=""></input>
    e. create an input hidden element with "id" having a specific pattern for storing column value
    f. pattern="col_val::"+gobal_counter
    g. <input type="hidden" id=pattern value=""></input>
4. gobal_counter ++
5. store the final global counter
    a. <input type="text" id="totalsearchcol"   id=pattern value=""></input>
    b. Input element to store the final string
    c. Input button to click and search
    d. On click event of the button the JAVASCRIPT function is called which in turn will call the service

Whenever we intend to represent a database entity in XML, we must remember that, we not only want to represent the information itself but also describe its context and specific properties (the so-called meta information). The above algorithm describes the showcase of underlying Database In that case, we also want to describe the way data is stored in the original RDB. A RDB has two components: structure and information. Our final XML document will have, accordingly, two parts, one that describes the structure of the RDB and another one to store the data contained by RDB. The XML skeleton of our final document will roughly resemble the one shown in Figure 4.6.

```
<?xml version="1.0" encoding="iso-8859-1"?>
<DB name="XXX" date="today">
<STRUCTURE>
...
</STRUCTURE>
<DATA>
...
</DATA>
    </DB>
```

Figure 4.6: DBML skeleton - general structure

The conversion of a RDB to XML must be able to tackle the following:

Structure: To fill the first part of the XML document we must access the structural information of the RDB and convert that information to an adequate XML structure. Each Database Management System has a particular way of storing this structural description of a database. The specific mediators will take care of this for each type of database.

Data: The transference of information from a RDB to XML is a more generic process. Almost every Database Management System allows the user to download the information in a database to a pure text file using pre-defined field and record separators. Therefore, the conversion problem to solve is the one of converting data from those text files to the second part of the final XML document. However, at the moment we have the mediators taking care of this too using common SQL queries that return the whole data available in a table.

The conversion is done by the mediators, one for each RDBMS. Mediators use Java Database Connectivity (JDBC) API to access the database structure information. When the JDBC driver for a specific RDBMS doesn't provide all the information needed or provides wrong information, specific methods are developed to extract the information directly from system tables. The translation scheme adopted by the mediators is the following:

Tables: Each table is mapped to an element named *TABLE* that has an attribute called *NAME*.

Columns: Each column will be mapped to a *COLUMN* element that also has a *NAME* attribute, where the column's name is saved. Other properties like the data type for the values of that column and the characteristic of being empty or not, are stored in attributes *TYPE* and *NULL* associated to the *COLUMN* element. As a table contains more than one column, it is necessary to include in the XML document another element, *COLUMNS*, to aggregate all the *COLUMN* instances.

Primary and Foreign Keys: Keys may be defined inside the table definition; so it will be described as a sub-element *TABLE*. An aggregation element, *KEYS*, has to be introduced to group the various keys in a table. The set of keys shall also be divided into Primary and Foreign Keys; so *PKEY* and *FKEY* were introduced as sub elements of *KEYS*. Moreover, a primary key in the relational model may be single (just one column) or compound (more than one column). To distinguish between the two cases, an attribute *TYPE* was associated to *PKEY* element, see Figure 4.7. As foreign keys (of single type) relate one table with another one, the *PKEY* element shall be associated using the attributes *IN* (identifier of the destination table) and *REF* (identifier of the linked fields in the destination table).

```
<TABLE NAME="Districts">
<COLUMNS>
<COLUMN NAME="code" TYPE="int" NULL="no"/>
...
</COLUMNS>
<KEYS>
<PKEY TYPE="simple">
<FIELD NAME=""/>
</PKEY>
<PKEY TYPE="compound">
<FIELD NAME=""/>
<FIELD NAME=""/>
</PKEY>
<KEY NAME="" REF=""/>
...
</KEYS>
</TABLE>
```

Figure 4.7: Translation skeleton

To illustrate the translation schema just described we will use the structure of a classical Products and Suppliers database that is composed of three tables: two tables are used to represent Products and Suppliers and a third table is used to implement the N:N relation that exists between the two. The primary key of tables Products and Suppliers is single and is stored in the column CODE, in both cases; there are no more keys. Concerning the third table, p2s, its primary key is of a composed type and the field elements are cod-p and cod-s; this table also has two foreign keys, cod-p and cod-s that establish the links to the two other tables. The result of the conversion is shown in Figure 4.8.

```
<?xml version="1.0" ?>
<DB>
<STRUCTURE>
<TABLE NAME="products">
<COLUMNS>
<COLUMN NAME="code" TYPE="nvarchar"
SIZE="10" NULL="no"/>
<COLUMN NAME="description" TYPE="nvarchar"
SIZE="50" NULL="no"/>
...
</COLUMNS>
<KEYS>
<PKEY TYPE="simple">
<FIELD NAME="code"/>
</PKEY>
</KEYS>
</TABLE>
<TABLE NAME="p2s">
<COLUMNS>
<COLUMN NAME="cod-p" TYPE="nvarchar"
SIZE="10" NULL="no"/>
<COLUMN NAME="cod-s" TYPE="nvarchar"
SIZE="10" NULL="no"/>
</COLUMNS>
<KEYS>
<PKEY TYPE="composite">
<FIELD NAME="cod-p"/>
```

```
<FIELD NAME="cod-s"/>
</PKEY>
<FKEY NAME="cod-p" IN="products"
REF="code"/>
<FKEY NAME="cod-s" IN="suppliers"
REF="code"/>
</KEYS>
</TABLE>
<TABLE NAME="suppliers">
<COLUMNS>
<COLUMN NAME="code" TYPE="nvarchar"
SIZE="10" NULL="no"/>
<COLUMN NAME="name" TYPE="nvarchar"
SIZE="60" NULL="no"/>
...
</COLUMNS>
<KEYS>
<PKEY TYPE="simple">
<FIELD NAME="code"/>
</PKEY>
</KEYS>
</TABLE>
</STRUCTURE>
<DATA>
...
</DATA>
    </DB>
```

Figure 4.8: The Products and Suppliers DB Structure translated into XML

Since this cache is supposed to work with any kind of database (we are talking about a database of databases, i.e. a metadatabase) we had to create an abstract relational model suitable for that. The model shown in Figure 4.9 is very similar to the ones used by database engines,

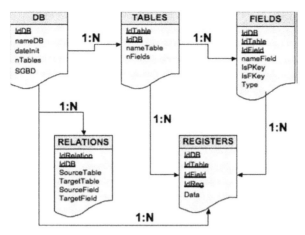

Figure 4.9: Database cache model

We have one table to store the database information, one to store table information, one for field information and another to store the data. All data items are converted to a textual form in order to be stored in this table. Although it may seem extremely inefficient this component works quite well in this prototype version.

We developed a navigator that enables users to browse the cached databases. Users may access and browse the database structure, access data items and navigate across relations. Figures 4.10, 4.11 and 4.12 present screenshots of this application.

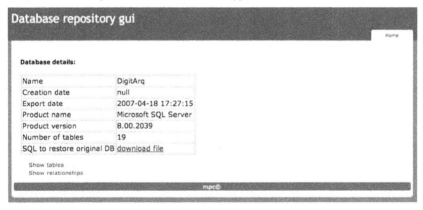

Figure 4.10: XML Database Browser - Basic Database Information

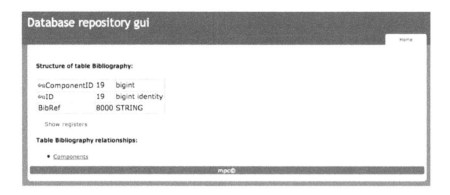

Figure 4.11: XML Database Browser - Columns Information

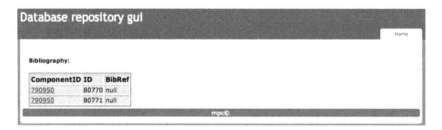

Figure 4.12: XML Database Browser - Registers Information

4.6 Block diagram of Information Query Retrieval system

Information Query Retrieval system was implemented using JAVA platform. Overall block diagram is shown in Figure 4.13.

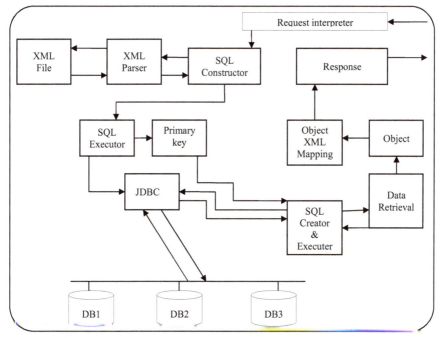

Figure 4.13: Block Diagram of Information Query Retrieval Systems.

The XML parsing and XSLT transformation is implemented using Apache Xerec and Xalan API. Object XML mapping was implemented with Castor API. The query interpreter processes the input search data. The SQL query creator perform the process of finding table info of the search columns and forming SQL queries and then the SQL query executer performs execution and storing required key value pair as discussed. After the primary key retrieval, data is retrieved based on the method selected.

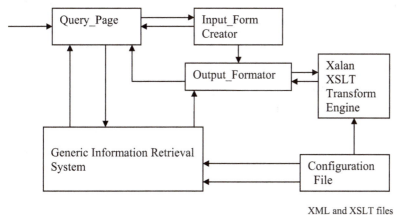

XML and XSLT files

Figure 4.14: Dynamic Query Interface Design.

If no global XML data is presents then data is stored in data objects. Based on the client's request the data is converted to xml using Object xml mapping concepts using Castor API. Web based dynamic query interface module was developed using JAVA platform and Apache Xalan as the xml transformation engine. Overall block diagram is shown in Figure 4.14.

4.7   Chapter Conclusion

This chapter explained the work involves in developing SOA information query retrieval system, the system is decomposed it in to following modules which need to be worked upon to create a loosely coupled system.

- Model for Relational Database Representation in XML Format, in this model XML format was preferred over the traditional delimiter separated file because of the ability of XML to show the hierarchical relations in an effective manner and also due to the flexibility to make changes without affecting the existing structure. An XML schema was design to represent the tables in a database and also the relations between the tables. Also we have tried to address the issue of heterogeneity in terms of column naming.

- Model to represent the input query, this model represents Input search query can either in a delimiter separated form or can be in XML form. We have implemented the Back-end Query Implementation, Logical Implementation of the back end module and Autosuggestion Feature for Taking Inputs from User. This model addresses the query execution time by rearranging the query by keeping the more specific part of the query first.

- Model to generate queries based on input conditions and querying, filtering, grouping across databases based on the input query and dispatch the output. The filtering and routing tasks were used as a test bed for our research in applying genetic algorithms leaning in Information Retrieval, in conjunction with the Probabilistic Information Retrieval. Model may also be viewed as a combination of the probabilistic retrieval model and a simple language model. For many of the experiments, our system has been demonstrated to provide superior effectiveness.

- Model to design the service interface to communicate with client application. This model represents the dynamic query interface to provide a loosely coupled system which interacts with the information retrieval system .This can be used as a plug in any web based client server model.

CHAPTER - 5

INFORMATION RETRIEVAL TECHNIQUES USING WEB LLD

In this chapter we have presented the use case, collaboration diagrams and Variable Length Coding/User Interface (VLC/UI) design process. The low level design supports for design the models proposed in chapter 4. The main goal of VLC/UI is to retrieval and display needed information from the source. Whereas the Low Level Design (LLD) has not yet clear for web based interactions. We proposed a new type of design using sequence diagram for web based design on browser side. UI also has to tell us how to complete the interfacing task. Say it uses Apache as web server to interact between Web-based main Graphical User Interface (GUI) on client side. The application of this concept is applicable to entire web based software development, Website development. Real time application like banking maintenance, library maintenance etc our concept gives more reliable result.

5.1 Overview of Low Level Design

Web servers are used for the different application in daily life like most software development, Website development, Library Management, Enterprises resource management, etc. the website or software uses GUI interface. For this application the web based GUI is most important interacting tool. According to literature survey number of approaches available for GUI designs. In this research let us discuss the web browser interface that is the GUI interface in detail, which can be the low level design. Here all the developers, managers, architects and each one who is directly or indirectly related with respect to web based GUI will think only for rich GUI. But they won't think for the detailed design of these interaction and synchronous or asynchronous communication through these components.

Here, it uses web server as and the GUI is a web-based design which includes applets using out of band connection, XSL files embedded with HTML files, XML and JavaScript (JS). This XSL and JS file connects to web server through HTTP connection where as applets connect through out of band connection.

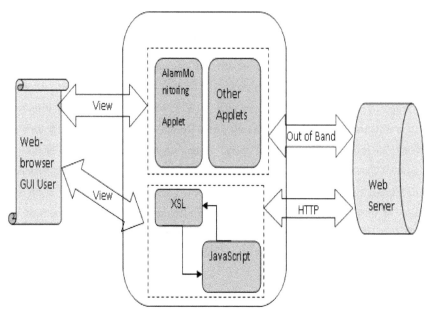

Figure 5.1: Web server clients GUI Low Level Design

The above Figure 5.1 depicts the General block diagram of Web server cum client GUI. Each block in the above figure is explained below.

- **Web browser GUI User:** Web browser GUI where user can view and operate. This user can be ordinary user.

- **Alarm Monitoring Applet:** If user wants to monitor alarms then they can use this applet. Alarm Monitoring applet, say appears as a pop-up when a user clicks on ALM-MON button in Web browser (this is one case or example). The alarms that occur can belong to any of the three severities like critical, major, and minor.

- **XSL:** The XSL(Extensible Stylesheet Language) block used to put .xsl files, this xsl files includes HTML tags inside to display the results read from XML files using XSLT(XSL Transformation) which were getting loaded to browser as the page loads.

- **JavaScript:** this block includes .js files which are used by XSL files. This JS files used to display Tree Structure, dynamic search, tabular form, pagination, etc. mainly JavaScript is used for even validation purpose. This Tree Structure, dynamic search, etc can be done through AJAX which is done through advanced JavaScript.

It explains the interaction is between the web browser GUI and web server. The applets work using out of band connection with the server. Here the detailed design includes the block diagram and the sequence diagrams. These sequence diagrams are more important while designing the detailed design of say web site which uses all components like HTML pages, XML files, XSL files and JavaScript's etc. Here each component is considering as one separate entity to draw sequence diagram or to understand the architecture of that current page.

5.2 Overview of UML Model Mappings

This research presents a model for describing the architecture of software-intensive systems, based on the use of multiple, concurrent views. This use of multiple views allows addressing separately the concerns of the various 'stakeholders' of the architecture: end-user, developers, systems engineers, project managers, etc., and to handle separately the functional and non functional requirements. Each of the five views is described, together with a notation to capture it. The views are designed using an architecture-centered, scenario driven, iterative development process.

Unified Modeling Language (UML) Model Mappings for Platform Independent User Interface Design describes while model based design of platform independent application logic has already shown significant success, the design of platform independent user interfaces still needs further investigation. Nowadays, user interface design is usually platform specific or based on C-level cross-platform libraries. In this research, we propose a *Model-driven architecture* (MDA) like design approach for user interfaces based on the transformation of UML models at different levels of abstraction. This enables platform independent design of user interfaces and a clear separation of UI and application logic design while enabling full use of native controls in the actual user interface implementation.

Designing User-Centered Web Applications in Web Time describes as designers struggle to develop Web applications "in Web time," they are under the added pressure of delivering usability. This research describes company's successful transformation to user-driven processes for designing e-commerce applications. Also offers strategies for introducing human factors methods into a reluctant development organization.

Developing Adaptive and Self-Managed Graphical User Interfaces describes in this research we present a structured approach for the analysis, specification and design of agent-based graphical user interfaces (GUI). A development process using design patterns as well as creative techniques is described. Performing interface design with our approach leads to a logical goal/task hierarchy that can be easily depicted by a society of agents. Furthermore an implicit partition of the GUI hidden in the given problem takes shape and gets connected with the particular agents.

5.3 Experimental Result

The methodology was tested initially without using these above features. Table 5.1 shows the time requires to understanding the detailed design of say website was pretty more in earlier design. But by using this approach the required time in the design process a well the problems which can occur in feature can be reduced. This in turn reduces the time.

	Time Before (in days)	Time After (in days)
Colleges	10	5
Company 1	12	4
Company 2	8	4

Table 5.1: Time required to designing the applications in days

In the Figure 5.2 it has been shown the time required to do the design of user interface for web based design and for knowledge transfer before and after use of this approach.

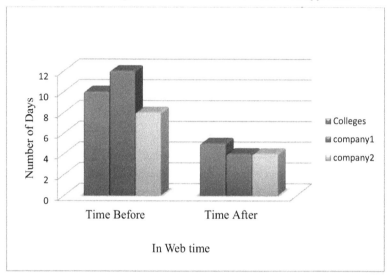

Figure 5.2: Experiment comparison bar chart

5.4   Discussion on Information Retrieval Systems

Model of IR Architecture proposed the development view, which describes the static organization of the software in its development environment to analyze the user interface design. Whereas UML Activity Diagrams: Detailing User Interface Navigation proposed how to use UML Activity Diagrams to capture and communicate the details of user interface navigation and functionality. But even using this concept it is very time consuming to design and understanding the whole concept with in limited time permit. In this concept it uses overall components which are directly or indirectly depended. Here we are using sequence diagram which makes the user to understand the overall design details very easily in less time duration.

5.4.1   Applet Interaction on Web Page

Applets will run on web page with the help of Java enabled web browsers. And applets wont connect with the same connection which is already existing one, applets creates its own out of band connection. This applet is Alarm Monitoring Applet where one can view various types of alarm with different severities like critical, major and minor.

1. User clicks on ALM-MON button in Web page main GUI it will call funAlmMon() method in JavaScript. The request STA-ALM-MON command goes to Web server as HTTP request, processes this request. Then STA-ALM-MON.xsl file starts the applet to monitor the alarm status.

2. Exception: Due to some reason exception occurred while calling alarm monitoring applet then it will be handled as shown in sequence diagram in ERROR block. The error related HTML page is send as response to client UI.

Sequence Diagram shown in Figure 5.3:

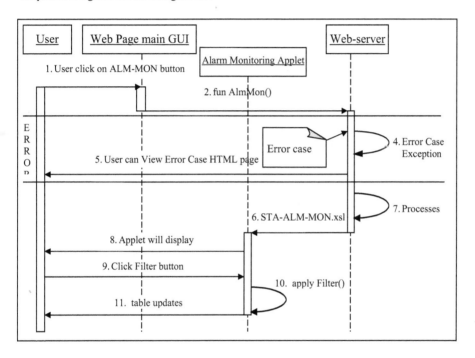

Figure 5.3: Sequence Diagram for Alarm Monitoring applet call

5.4.2 Alarm Monitoring Applet Structure

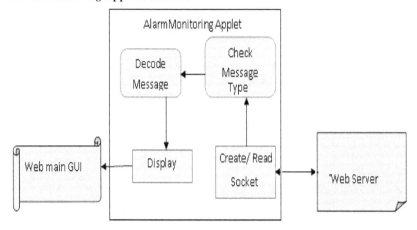

Figure 5.4: Low Level/Detailed Design of Alarm Monitoring applets

The operation of Alarm Monitoring applet is show in blocks as in Figure 5.4 Where Web main GUI is the place where the user interacts. It contains even four internal modules to read the input from the user, process it and send to Web Server through Create/Read Socket block.

Sequence Diagram of working of Alarm Monitoring Applet:

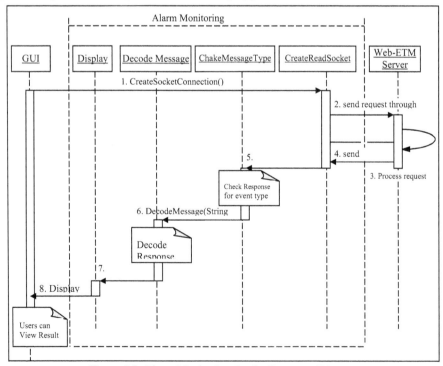

Figure 5.5: Alarm Monitoring Applet Sequence Diagram

5.4.3 Tree Based Command Selection Window

Tree Based Command Selection detailed design includes Web-based GUI and JavaScript file to display in tree structure as shown in Figure 5.6. In this tree structure for example the branches are Configuration, Software, Fault, Performance and Diagnosis. Each branch contains the leaves as their commands. New Java script needs to be written to support Tree structure.

First user login the Web site,

1. Web browser main GUI page will display
2. Go to command window in the main page and one can see the commands in tree like structured. Click on any branch of the tree.

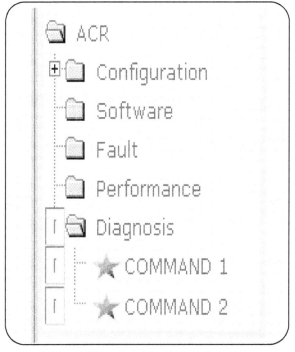

Figure 5.6: Tree Structure

1. This tree structure will be created by using Tree JavaScript file. It calls the loadXML(..) method to search file form Web page factory created by Web server.
2. It read the command list from the XML file.
3. When user clicks on branch in command window to check the list of commands.
4. gFld(..) JavaScript method is called to load the commands
5. Tree JavaScript loads the commands
6. And load to command window of main page
7. User can view the list.

Below sequence Figure 5.7 shows the general flow in Tree Base Command Selection.

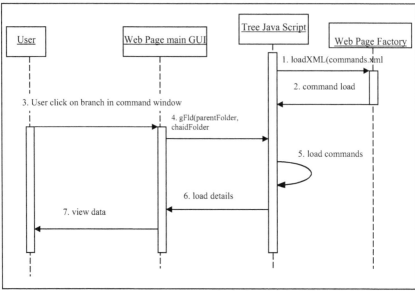

Figure 5.7: Sequence Diagram for Tree Based Command Selection

5.4.4 Search Tab for Dynamic Command Search

Dynamic Command Search is the new option it consist of text box and list box in it. OnKeyUp JavaScript method is called to check the commands related to particular branch. Wrong key press check is also taken care.

1. Click on the Search Tab in the command window then user can view Dynamic Search tab as in Figure 5.9.
2. DyanmicSearch() method is called in JavaScript
3. loadXML(commands.xml) JavaScript method is called while loading
4. loads all commands to an array
5. Dynamic Search Tab loads and user can view the same
6. If user presses any key
7. OnKeyUp() JavaScript method is called. This JavaScript checks the key pressed and checks the commands starting letter/word with input letter/word and gets the result
8. The result is send to list box in search tab
9. User can view the commands

The sequence figure 5.8 is shown below.

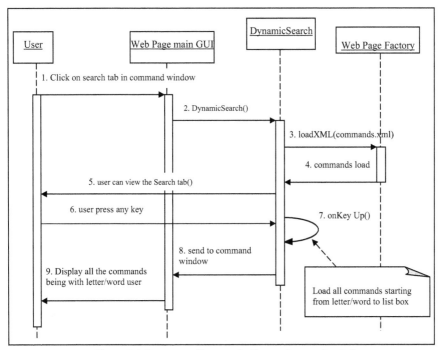

Figure 5.8 Sequence diagram for Dynamic search window

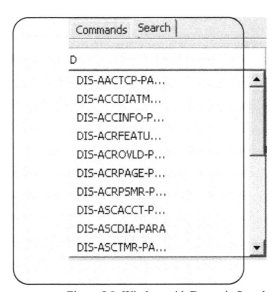

Figure 5.9: Window with Dynamic Search

Exception: If user presses wrong key then an alert box will display with "Wrong Key Pressed". The sequence diagram is shown in Figure 5.10.

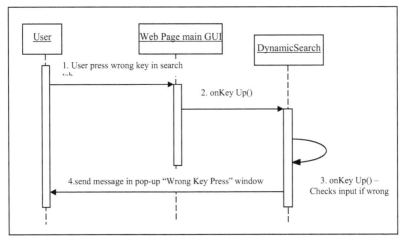

Figure 5.10: Sequence Diagram of Dynamic Search for error handling

1. If user presses the wrong key
2. The request will go to JavaScript
3. Here it checks for the write key press. If it is wrong it will send a alert to main page
4. The alert pop-up will be displayed to user by telling wrong key.

The new Web-LLD has been used with success on several minor and major projects with or without some alternations in the underlying technologies. It actually made the stakeholders or the designers to construct or design the detailed architecture in minimum amount of time. And even someone who have not involved in the design can easily understand the system very easily.

5.5   Chapter conclusion

*   In this chapter we have explained only the use case, collaboration diagrams, and VLC/UI design process. The main goal of VLC/UI is to retrieval and display needed information from the source. Whereas the Low Level Design (LLD) has not yet clear for web based interactions.

*   In this research we implemented the web browser interface that is the GUI interface in detail, which can be the low level design. Here all the developers, managers, architects and each one who is directly or indirectly related with respect to web based GUI will think only for rich GUI. But they won't think for the detailed design of these interaction and synchronous or asynchronous communication through these components.

*   The time requires to understanding the detailed design of say website was pretty more in earlier design. But by using this approach the required time in the design process a well the problems which can occur in feature can be reduced. This in turn reduces the time.

*   Applets will run on web page with the help of Java enabled web browsers. And applets wont connect with the same connection which is already existing one, applets creates its own out

of band connection. This applet is a Alarm Monitoring Applet where one can view various types of alarm with different severities like critical, major, and minor.

- Tree Based Command Selection detailed design includes Web-based GUI and JavaScript file to display in tree structure. In this tree structure for example the branches are Configuration, Software, Fault, Performance and Diagnosis. Each branch contains the leaves as their commands. New Java script needs to be written to support Tree structure.

CHAPTER - 6
PERFORMANCE OF INFORMATION RETRIEVAL SYSTEM USING WEB SERVICES

In this chapter, we present the implementation of system simulation, prototype system and the design for experiments to study the performance of Information Retrieval (IR) systems. The models proposed in chapter 4 is outperforms the experimental results. The prototype of information retrieval system is based on query, an existing, unified IR system. We have implemented a flexible simulation model to serve as a platform for analyzing performance issues given a wide variety of system parameters and configurations. We validate the accuracy of our simulation model using prototype. We present a series of experiments that are designed to measure system utilization and identify bottlenecks. We vary numerous system parameters, such as the number of applications, databases & user collections, number of terms per query, response time and system load to generalize our results for other distributed IR systems models [140-145].

Information retrieval systems using web services are increasingly being used on larger databases and by more users. Current systems allow users to connect to a multiple databases either locally or perhaps on another machine. The resource demands limit the performance of IR systems especially as the size of text collections and the number of applications increase. Service oriented architecture (SOA) computing offers a solution to these problems. Systems based on distributed architectures can use resources more efficiently by spreading work across a network of workstations and by enabling parallel computation.

An IR system is an ideal application to distribute across a network of workstations. The amount of information available and the number of people accessing data over networks is rapidly increasing. To meet future demands, IR system must provide concurrent, efficient access to multiple databases collections located on remote locations. However, due to the mix of I/O and CPU intensive operations, IR systems present unique problems for distributed system designers. The disparity between I/O and processor speeds exacerbates these problems. Another concern is network traffic, since the amount of data transferred over the network by IR system fluctuates considerably.

The focus of our research is to analyze the performance of SOA for information retrieval system architecture. A change to different system parameters (e.g., the number of applications and database collections) affects response time, throughput, and resource utilization. During our investigation we will identify potential bottlenecks and study the effects of various architectures and parameters. Our goal is to use resources efficiently by maximizing parallelism and ensuring scalability. Also, we believe it is important to maintain the effectiveness, in terms of recall and precision of Internet based SOA for IR system.

6.1   Information Retrieval System using Web Services

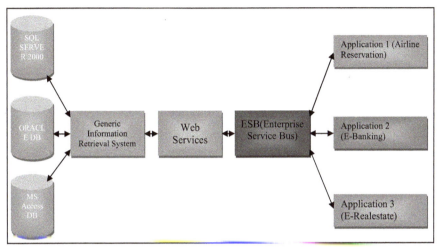

Figure 6.1: Basic architecture of information retrieval system

We have implemented a prototype of information query retrieval system that is based on SOA; an inference network. The system adopts a variation of the client-server paradigm consisting of a set of applications connected to a set of retrieval databases through a central administration process. The basic architecture is illustrated in Figure 6.1.

The Enterprise service Bus (ESB) is the user interface to the databases. Clients initiate the work performed in the system by sending commands to the database servers. The commands include the retrieval operations such as query evaluation and document retrieval. The client also determines the set of text collections to search for query operations. Web services are the retrieval engine. Generic information retrieval system server represents a multiple open database that is selected at start-up time. All retrieval operations take place at the generic information retrieval system server. There are three types of generic information retrieval system servers: query, document and integrated. A query server only performs query operations, a document server only performs document retrieval operations and an integrated server performs both document retrieval and query evaluation operations. The ESB is the administrator between the clients and generic information retrieval system servers. Multiple clients and generic information retrieval system servers may be connected to the same connection server. The connection server is a loosely coupled and lightweight process that manages the work between the user interface and retrieval engine. All messages passed between the clients and generic information retrieval system servers must go through the web services. Messages are placed in a queue until the generic information retrieval system server is available to process new operations. The ESB also maintains a limited amount of state information about current operations and available databases.

6.2 Models Designed for Information Retrieval System

The proposed IR system has been design and developed using the following modules which need to be worked upon to create a loosely coupled system.

5. Represent the underlying relational database in a generic form.

6. Represent the input query.

7. Generate queries based on input conditions and querying, filtering, grouping across databases based on the input query and dispatch the output.

8. Design the service interface to communicate with client application.

6.3 Simulation of IR System Model

A simulation technique of the above IR system modules provides an effective and flexible platform for analyzing large and complex distributed systems. We can quickly change inputs, run experiments and analyze results without making numerous changes to large amounts of code. Furthermore, simulation models allow us to easily define very large systems and examine results in a controlled environment.

We have written a simulation of system model of our SOA for information retrieval system. The model is designed to be simple, yet contain enough details to accurately represent the important features of the system. The work modeled by the simulation represents the activities performed by an actual retrieval system. The model is driven by empirical measurements obtained from generic information retrieval system server an existing IR system. Although the model is based upon generic information retrieval system server, it is parameterized in order to easily model variations of our own system and other retrieval systems.

6.4 Simulation Toolkit

Our simulator is built upon the MATLAB simulation library and Eclipse spring IDE. Eclipse spring is a process-oriented discrete-event simulation language based on the JAVA programming language. The process-oriented nature of the MATLAB simulation language allows the structure of the simulator to closely reflect the actual system. MATLAB contains a set of data structures and library routines that manage user-created simulation objects. A simulation object defines an activity (i.e., a process), a queue (i.e., a resource), or a statistic record. The simulator models the major components of our system (i.e., the clients, connection server, and generic information retrieval system servers) as MATLAB processes. Processes simulate the activities of the real system by requesting services from resources. A process that requests a resource executes when the resource is available. Otherwise, the process suspends until the resource is available. The processes synchronize via a set of

MATLAB message passing library routines. Processes that are waiting for messages suspend until the appropriate message is received.

Eclipse spring IDE provides convenient mechanisms to model resources. Each resource is defined as a queue and a set of servers. When a resource is requested by a process, it is assigned to an available server. If the server is not available, the request is queued until a server becomes free. Our model defines a CPU as a resource with multiple database servers. The queuing discipline used by the resource mimics an actual processor. Each request is serviced without delay, but as the number of requests increases, the remaining service time for each request increases. For example if two processes request the CPU at the same time for one second then it takes a total of two seconds for each process to complete. The simulator models a disk as a resource with one server which uses a First in First out (FIFO) queuing discipline. Each request is serviced without interruption when the server becomes available. If the disk is not available, the simulator places the request at the end of the queue. The network resource is limited by the amount of data that can be transmitted at any time rather than the number of requests that it can handle. A user parameter constrains the bandwidth of the network. The model defines the network as a resource with servers for each of the processes created. Thus, each process may send a message at any time. The simulator queues new requests when the bandwidth would be exceeded.

6.5   Information Retrieval Query Evaluation

Users supply parameters to construct the artificial parameters generated by the simulator. The parameters include:

- Distribution of the number of terms in a query.
- Distribution of the query term frequencies.
- Maximum term frequency in the text collection.
- Number of queries to generate.

The simulator accurately reflects the operations performed by the prototype. That is, once a query is generated it is sent to the connection server over the network and the connection server is responsible for routing the message to the appropriate generic information retrieval system servers. The client receives a ranked list of matching documents and then obtains summary information about the documents.

6.6   Simulation of Information Retrieval System Parameters

To accurately model an IR system, we have analyzed the generic information retrieval system and measured the time the resources used for each operation. Empirical measurements rather than an analytical model drive the activities performed in the simulator. Creating a full analytical model requires too many simplifying assumptions to make an accurate model of a complex information retrieval system.

In this section, we first describe the collections of applications used to obtain resource measurements. We also describe the measurements for each of the activities performed by the prototype. The measurements include:

- Query evaluation time.
- Document retrieval time.
- Summary retrieval time.
- Connection server time.
- Time to merge results.
- Network time.

We obtained measurements using aDECsystem-5000/240 (MIPSR3000 clocked at 40MHz) workstation running Ultrix V4.2A (Rev. 47) with 64MB of memory and 300MB of swap space. To minimize the effects of other users we ran all tests during the evening when the system load was very light.

6.6.1   Text Collections Used to Obtain Measurements

We examined several different text collections and query sets to obtain measurements used in the simulation. The text collections are.

- Airline Reservation
- E-Real estate
- E-Banking

Table 6.1 lists statistics about the text collections and query sets. Airline Reservation is a large heterogeneous collection of full-text databases and abstracts used in the reservation system. The documents in the collection come from a variety of open sources including online reservation, broker reservation center, and authorized counters. The average document size is not large but the sizes of the documents vary from 100 bytes to 1 MB. The Airline Reservation collection includes a set of 50 queries created automatically from reservation topics 51-100. The queries consist of English text and do not contain any structured operators.

The information collection contains the text of the E-Banking. The documents in the collection summarize of the day's events from E-Banking. The size of the documents range from 1K to 700K and the average document size are large. We included this collection since it is a database that is accessible over the Internet and we were able to obtain the user query traces. We examined the query logs five year data to obtain realistic query statistics. Interestingly, people searching the database typically enter small queries, usually only 1 or 2 words and never more than 8 words. This contrasts with the other query sets that contain long queries.

Collection	Collection Statistics						Query Statistics	
	Size (MB)	No. of Documents	Avg. Doc Size (KB)	No. of Postings	Max Term Frequency		No. of Queries	Avg. No. of Terms
E-Banking	1980	520887	2.9	159571494	654658		80	47.1
E-Real estate	2.8	3904	0.8	185967	5208		70	30.7
Airline Reservation	5.6	45378	18.7	58078407	814849		5141	6

Table 6.1 Collection and Query Set Statistics

The E-Real estate document collection consists of small abstracts from the communications of the E-Real estate. This collection is an older test collection consisting of a small number of homogeneous documents. The collection is only 2MB and the average size of the documents is small. The E-Real estate collection also includes a set of 50 English text queries. Again, no structured operators appear in the queries.

6.6.2 Query Evaluation Measurements

In information retrieval system, a query operation consists of creating a query network, evaluating the query network on the document network, and ranking the documents that match the query. Since the process is quite complicated, we empirically measured the time required to evaluate a query using information retrieval system rather than creating a complex analytical model. We found that the evaluation time is very strongly related to the number of terms in the query and the frequency of each of the terms. Figure 6.2 shows a scatter plot which compares query length versus evaluation time for each query in the Airline Reservation query set. The correlation is very high, .96, indicating a strong linear association between query length and query evaluation time. Figure 6.3 shows the relation between term frequency and evaluation time. Again, the correlation coefficient, .95, indicates a very strong association. To collect this data, we measured evaluation times for individual terms with different term frequencies.

The Table 6.2 describes the performance of evaluation time and number of queries which will vary from small query to larger queries.

SL No.	Number of Query	Evaluation Time in Sec
1	2	20
2	7	25
3	8	50
4	9	60

5	10	90
6	5	75
7	7	80
8	40	150
9	45	130
10	30	30
11	80	250
12	30	100
13	20	56
14	15	45
15	5	45
16	6	30
17	10	46
18	15	70
19	25	74
20	25	80
21	60	155
22	30	78
23	40	100
24	38	104
25	50	105
26	45	150
27	50	150
28	25	99
29	15	75
30	16	85
31	20	90

Table 6.2: Query Sets per evaluation time

The simulation model contains a distribution of evaluation times based upon the term frequency. We measured the time to evaluate the individual terms with information retrieval system. Given a query that is internally represented as a list of term frequency values, the evaluation time is the sum of the times for evaluating the individual terms in the query. The data in Figure 6.2 indicates that this simple model reflects the time to perform query evaluation.

The Table 6.3 illustrate the term frequency and evaluation time which is obtained from the simulation.

Sl No.	Term Frequency	Evaluation Time
1	10000	0.2
2	20000	0.4
3	30000	0.5
4	40000	0.5
5	50000	0.6
6	50000	0.8
7	55000	0.9
8	30000	1
9	40000	1.4
10	50000	1.5
11	55000	1.7
12	60000	2.3
13	66000	2.5
14	70000	2
15	80000	2
16	90000	2.8
17	100000	3
18	110000	3.5
19	150000	4
20	170000	2
21	100000	2
22	125500	6
23	130000	3
24	134000	2.5
25	150000	5
26	157000	5.4
27	160000	4.3
28	170000	5
29	180000	4
30	185000	4.5
31	190000	3

32	200000	6
33	250000	6.5
34	275000	7
35	280000	7.5
36	290000	6.5
37	300000	8
38	350000	8.5
39	400000	12
40	425000	11
41	450000	10
42	470000	14
43	500000	15
44	600000	18
45	600000	10

Table 6.3: Term Frequency and Evaluation Time

We validated the query model used by the simulation against the actual system. Figure 6.4 shows that the simulation model is close but does not exactly reflect the actual system, especially for large queries. However, there is a strong correlation between the simulation times and actual times. The difference between the times is due to the simple model used by the simulation. The actual retrieval process implemented by information retrieval system is quite complex and difficult to describe using a simple model. Although it is not perfect, the general trend of the model is accurate. (Using a prototype and a model enables us to do this type of validation. We need to examine the actual retrieval process in greater detail to add more features to the simulation model.

The following Table 6.4 indicates the evaluation time and queries that has been simulated with sufficient set of queries. Evaluation time varies from minimum to maximum.

Sl No.	Evaluation Time	Queries
1	20	10
2	25	11
3	25	12
4	30	13
5	30	14
6	32	14
7	34	16

8	35	30
9	40	35
10	45	35
11	46	32
12	48	45
13	100	10
14	120	2
15	125	3
16	150	4
17	155	0
18	175	2
19	190	3
20	200	1
21	220	1
22	221	1
23	250	0
24	300	0

Table 6.4: Evaluation Time and Queries

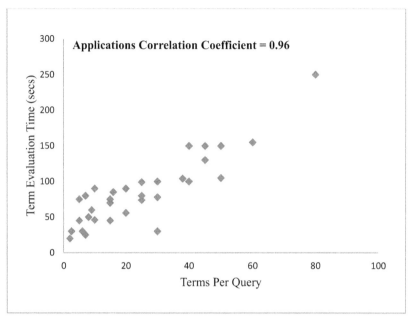

Figure 6.2: Query Lengths vs. Evaluation Time

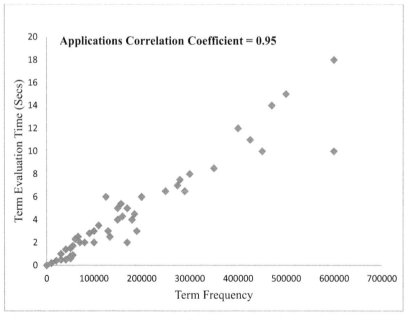

Figure 6.3: Term Frequency vs. Evaluation Time

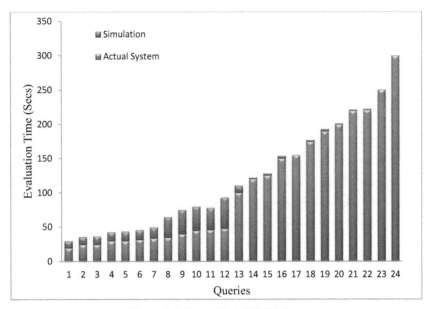

Figure 6.4: Query Model Validations

6.7   Simulation of Information Retrieval System Configuration

A user defines the architecture of the distributed information retrieval system using a simple command language. A configuration file contains the commands and the simulator reads this file at start-up time. Command line options may also be used to define certain aspects of the architecture and these options override any commands in the configuration file. The command line options allow users to easy run the simulator in batch mode by using a single configuration file and changing the command line options for each simulation. For example, if an experiment tests the effect of the number of clients, then a single configuration file defines the architecture and a command line option specifies the number of clients [146-150]. The command language supports a rich and flexible set of commands for specifying different distributed architectures. Table 6.5 describes the set of commands that define the different processes and resources used by the simulation. Each of these commands expects a parameter which is either a constant value or an expression evaluated when the file is read.

Category	Command	Description
Processes	`clients`	Number of clients
	`conn_servers`	Number of connection servers
	`db_servers`	Number of database servers
Resources	`Cpus`	Number of processors
	`Disks`	Number of disks
	`Lans`	Number of local area networks

Objects	Machines	Number of hosts
	Database	Number of text collections

Table 6.5: Definition Commands

Table 6.6 describes the commands that assign properties and attributes to the simulation objects. The parameters depend upon the actual command. The configuration file allows users to provide parameters as constant values or symbolic values evaluated when the simulator reads the file. A user creates system architecture by assigning processes to resources. Also, users may assign various attributes to resources or combine several resources creating a larger object. For examine, a machine object is a combination of the CPU, disk, and network resources. A user creates a complete distributed architecture by defining connections between the different processes.

Command	Properties
Conn_server	Machine assigned to connection server
Client	Machine assigned to client
DB_server	Machine, database, and type of server
Machine	CPU, Disk, and LAN that create a machine
Lan	Bandwidth of network in MB/s
Database	Size of collection, No. of documents, Avg. size of documents
Connect	Define connections between processes
Queries	Define attributes of queries

Table 6.6: Property Commands

6.8   Experimental Methodology of IR

We describe the experiments we will conduct in order to analyze the performance of our system, identify potential bottlenecks, and to create a scalable system. We first describe our experiments that analyze system utilization. We briefly discuss several other types of experiments are as follows.

6.8.1   System Utilization

We designed these initial sets of experiments to measure the utilization of the different resources in the distributed system under varying conditions.

6.8.2   Fixed Parameters for System Utilization

In the initial experiments, the system architecture closely matches the prototype client-server version of information retrieval system. We must fix several parameters throughout these experiments to match the architecture of prototype system. We fix other parameters to reduce the total number of experiments performed. We will explore the effects of varying these parameters in future experiments.

The fixed parameters are:

- Functionality of processes (*e.g.,* clients, connection server, database servers)
- Connectivity between clients and database servers
- Size of text collections
- Network speed

6.8.3   Information Exchange and Query Retrieval System

The Information Exchange and Query Retrieval System architecture defines a set of clients, a multiple connection server and a set of databases servers. We described the basic components of the prototype client-server information retrieval system. The simulator allocates each of these components to its own host to eliminate the effects of competing processes and to measure the overall parallelism in the system. Each host contains its own processor, memory and secondary storage. A local area network with a bandwidth of 10 MBs connects all hosts.

Each databases server processes both query and document retrieval operations. The size of the text collection managed by each server is one GB. The size of the collection influences the frequency of the 12 terms in the queries. We analyzed the Airline Reservation document collection to determine the average size of a document and the average size of the summary information for each document. The document retrieval and summary information operations use these parameters. Upon initialization, each client connects to a random number of databases servers and the connections remain throughout the simulation. The process of connecting to a random number of database servers simulates the actions performed by actual users. That is, a typical user will choose to search some set of available text collections, or a single collection that is distributed over a set of machines. Connecting to all the available database servers or only one of the databases is probably rare.

6.8.4   Parameters for IR System Utilization

We analyze system utilization by running many experiments which vary several important parameters. The parameters affect system performance and are often variable in actual systems. We will determine the effects of these parameters on system performance by using the simulator. We provide a description of the experiment parameters listed below in the following sections.

- Number of Applications
- Number of Database servers.
- Terms per query.
- Distribution of terms in queries.

- Number of documents that match query.
- Think Rate.
- Documents retrieved.
- Summary information operations.

Number of Applications/ Database Servers

Measuring the effect of increasing the number of Applications and Database servers provides insight into identifying when each of the processes and resources become overburdened.

As the number of applications increases, the amount of total work performed in the system increases. The connection servers must handle more messages and the database servers perform more retrieval operations. Also, the amount of data transmitted across the network increases. If the clients each connect to distinct database servers, then the parallelism of the system improves since the components can operated concurrently. However, if several applications connect to the same database servers then the effect on the system is unclear, but obviously performance will degrade somewhat due to contention of resources. Regardless of the connections, the performance of the connection server decreases as the number of applications increases. It is also unclear when the performance degradation will become intolerable.

The database servers handle query evaluation and document retrieval operations. These operations are both CPU and I/O intensive. In general, the document retrieval operations occur much more quickly than query operations. Increasing the number of database servers in the system has a slightly different effect than increasing the number of applications. Each database server is located on its own processor and operates independently from the others. Any effect on performance caused by adding additional database servers is due to additional connections to the server, i.e., the additional connections create extra contention for resources and cause more messages to be passed between the components. In the simulation, as the number of database servers increases, the number of connections between the Applications and connection servers increases causing more contention for resources. Thus, increasing the number of Database servers increases the total amount of work performed by the system.

We will test configurations using **2**, **3**, **4**, **8**, **30**, **60**, and **120** applications and database servers. Baseline comparison architecture consists of three applications and three database servers. The other values provide meaningful comparisons between small and large configurations.

Terms per Query

There are several reasons to consider the performance effects caused by varying the number of terms per query. First, the time to evaluate a query is strongly related to the length of the query. In addition, the length of queries entered into a retrieval system varies significantly from one or two keywords to over 20.

Table 6.7 shows the occurrences of term query for the E- Banking application which will be simulated based on the more number of occurrences over term query.

Sl No.	Term Per Query	Occurrences
1	1	40
2	2	35
3	3	15
4	4	5
5	5	2
6	7	1
7	8	0
8	9	0

Table 6.7: Occurrences and Term query for E- Banking

The performance of the airline reservation illustrated in the Table 6.8 which will describe the simulation of occurrences over the term per query.

Sl No.	Term Per Query	Occurrences
1	16	27
2	23	24
3	30	17
4	37	17
5	44	5
6	51	3
7	58	0
8	65	2
9	72	0
10	79	0
11	86	0
12	93	0
13	100	2

Table 6.8: Occurrences and Term query for Airline Reservation

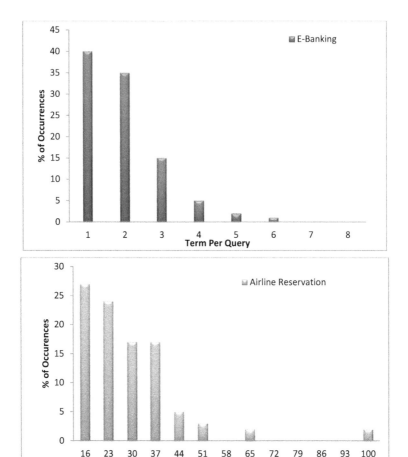

Figure 6.5: Query Length Distribution

Figure 6.5 shows the query length distribution for the E-Banking and Airline Reservation query sets. Notice that, even though the two query sets are very different, the shapes of the distributions are very similar. We use this information to create the synthetic queries.

Distribution of Terms in Queries

Zip documented the widely accepted distribution of term frequencies in text collections based upon empirical measurements. In contrast, the distribution of term frequencies in queries is more difficult to characterize and researchers do not agree on a commonly accepted distribution. Figure 6.6 shows the query term frequency distributions for our query sets. The shapes of the distributions for the three query sets are very similar. The difference between the three distributions is due to the size of the text collections.

Comparison and deference's of the different applications is examined in the simulator and obtains the various occurrences over the term query is shown in Table 6.9.

Sl No.	Term Frequency	Occurrences		
		Airline Reservation	E-Real estate	E-Banking
1	1	4	0	0
2	10	6	2	1
3	50	10	3	1
4	100	15	4	1
5	150	18	6	2
6	200	22	8	2
7	250	25	10	2
8	500	30	12	3
9	750	40	14	4
10	1000	60	16	5
11	1500	80	18	6
12	2000	90	20	8
13	3000	90	25	12
14	6000	100	33	16
15	8000	100	40	20
16	10000	100	50	25
17	15000	100	60	35
18	50000	100	70	45
19	100000	100	80	60
20	150000	100	90	80
21	1000000	100	95	90
22	1500000	100	95	95

Table 6.9: Term frequency and occurrence for different applications

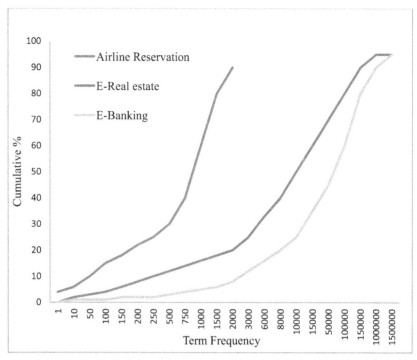

Figure 6.6: Query Term Frequency Distributions

The Airline Reservation text collection is the largest, so the distribution is shifted to the right indicating that the terms used in the queries appear more frequency. As the figure shows, the shape of the collection term frequency and the query term frequency distributions are very different. The frequency of most of the query terms is somewhere in the middle of the text collection distribution. Terms that occurs very infrequently or very frequently in the text collection rarely occurs in queries.

Number of Documents That Match Query

The IR system returns a sorted list of matching documents *ids* from the database servers. To reduce the number of matching documents returned, users usually specify a maximum value. The number of documents returned has an effect on network traffic and processing by the connection server and database servers. We will experiment with returning the top **1000** and top **100** documents [151-154].

Think Rate

In the simulated workload, "thinking" occurs after receiving summary information and after retrieving a document. Thinking represents the time users need to look at the results of their requests. The amount of thinking performed after each retrieval operation can have a significant effect on overall performance. When a client is thinking, it remains idle and other processes are allowed access to the system resources. Clients initiate operations more frequently and there is more contention for resources when they think time is short. On the other hand, system resources may remain idle if they think time is too long.

It is important to understand under what conditions system resources become saturated or underutilized. In the experiments, we will change the time spent thinking to study this effect. The think time after a summary information operation will be **30**, **90**, or **240** seconds. The think time after a document retrieval operation will be **60**, **180**, or **480** seconds.

Document Retrieval and Summary Information

During our experiments, we will vary the number of summary information operations and the number of documents received after each query is evaluated. These operations are similar since they both involve retrieving documents. Document retrieval operations are I/O intensive, but, in general, take less time than query operations. When very few documents are retrieved, query evaluation time will dominate the performance of the distributed system. When the client process retrieves many documents, the effects of the operations will be more balanced. As more documents are retrieved, more time is spent thinking. This idle time also has an effect on the system since it frees system resources.

We categorize the number of summary operations and documents retrieved that the client performs into three groups. These groups represent workloads seen in practice and each group represents a range of summary information or document operations. The number of operations to perform is randomly chosen from the following ranges: **1-5**, **8-12**, and **15-20**. For example, in the first range, the client performs between 1 and 5 summary information and document retrieval operations.

6.9 Discussions

In this research work presented an approach and implementation of a SOA for querying retrieval system which can used for querying and analysis with each module being loosely coupled with other. By reviewing the results and analysis of all the above mentioned models, it is found that SOA for IR outperforms all the existing models. Hence, it is conclude that the SOA can be used in the design and development of information retrieval system.

As per the formal problem definition mentioned in introduction chapter the proposed models are performs information retrieval in better way for designing the context independent and configurable module design. Service oriented model design where each module behaves independent of each other. Performs generic modules to perform querying and analysis on an underlying relational database. Dynamic query interface module which can be plugged in to any web based program to interact with system.

LIST OF ABBREVIATIONS

ADB	:	Axis2 Data Binding
AJAX	:	Asynchronous JavaScript and XML
API	:	Application Program Interface
ASMF	:	Action Script Messaging Format
AXIOM	:	Axis2 Object Model
BPEL	:	*Business Process Execution Language*
BPM	:	Business Process Management
CORBA	:	Common Object Request Broker
DBMS	:	Database Management System
DCOM	:	Distributed Component Object Model
EJB	:	Enterprise Java Beans
ESB	:	Enterprise Service Bus
FDBMS	:	Federated Database Management Systems
GUI	:	Graphical User Interface
HTML	:	Hyper Text Markup Language
HTTP	:	Hypertext Transfer Protocol
IR	:	Information Retrieval
JAXB	:	Java API for XML Binding
JAXR	:	Java API for XML Registry
JDBC-WS	:	Java Database Connectivity web services
LLD	:	Low Level Design
MTOM	:	Message Transmission Optimization Mechanism
OASIS	:	Advancement of Structured Information Standards
ORB	:	Object Request Broker
OSI	:	Open Systems Interconnection
POJO	:	Plain Old Java Objects
QoS	:	Quality of Service
RDF	:	Resource Description Framework
RDQL	:	*RDF Data Query Language*
RMI	:	Remote Method Invocation

RPC	:	Remote Procedure Call
SaaS	:	Software as a Service
SAML	:	Security Assertion Markup Language
SCA	:	Service Component Architecture
SMTP	:	Simple Mail Transfer Protocol
SOA	:	Service Oriented Architecture
SOAP	:	Simple Object Access Protocol
SOMF	:	Service-Oriented Modeling Framework
SOX	:	Sarbanes Oxley
SQL	:	Schema Structured Query Language
TCP/IP	:	*Transmission Control Protocol/Internet Protocol*
UDDI	:	Universal Description Discovery and Integration
UML	:	*Unified Modeling Language*
VLC	:	Variable Length Coding
W3C	:	World Wide Web Consortium
WSBPEL	:	Web Services Business Process Execution Language
WS-CDL	:	Web Services Choreography Description Language
WSDL	:	Web Services Descriptive Language
WSDM	:	Web Services for Distributed Management
WS-RM	:	Web Service Reliable Messaging
XML	:	Extensible Markup language
XOP	:	Optimized Packaging
XSLT	:	Extensible Style sheet Language

Publisher: Eliva Press SRL

Email: info@elivapress.com

Eliva Press is an independent publishing house established for the publication and dissemination of academic works all over the world. Company provides high quality and professional service for all of our authors.

Our Services:
Free of charge, open-minded, eco-friendly, innovational.

-Free standard publishing services (manuscript review, step-by-step book preparation, publication, distribution, and marketing).
-No financial risk. The author is not obliged to pay any hidden fees for publication.
-Editors. Dedicated editors will assist step by step through the projects.
-Money paid to the author for every book sold. Up to 50% royalties guaranteed.
-ISBN (International Standard Book Number). We assign a unique ISBN to every Eliva Press book.
-Digital archive storage. Books will be available online for a long time. We don't need to have a stock of our titles. No unsold copies. Eliva Press uses environment friendly print on demand technology that limits the needs of publishing business. We care about environment and share these principles with our customers.
-Cover design. Cover art is designed by a professional designer.
-Worldwide distribution. We continue expanding our distribution channels to make sure that all readers have access to our books.

www.elivapress.com